Nick Hornby

About a Boy

Teacher's Manual

by

Peter Bruck

Cornelsen

Contents

Nick Hornby
About a Boy
Teacher's Manual

Erarbeitet von
Peter Bruck

Verlagsredaktion
Neil Porter

Herstellung
Petra Jentschke

Herausgeber der Cornelsen Senior English Library
Prof. Dr. Albert-Reiner Glaap

www.cornelsen.de

2. Auflage, 3. Druck 2007

Druck: CS-Druck CornelsenStürtz, Berlin

ISBN 978-3-464-37165-7

Inhalt gedruckt auf säurefreiem Papier aus nachhaltiger Forstwirtschaft.

Introduction

Reasons for Reading *About a Boy*

Nick Hornby's novel *About a Boy* has become a great success in the English-language classroom. There are various reasons why it is such a hit:

- *An interesting story dealing with a familiar theme:*

On one level, the novel depicts the emotional and spiritual growth of both the 12-year-old Marcus and the 36-year-old bachelor Will Freeman. Marcus grows from being an innocent and unconventional boy into a normal teenager, while Will develops from a self-centred and carefree person into an emotionally mature and caring adult. In this sense, *About a Boy* stands in the wake of the classical educational novel; the theme of growing-up which students have dealt with in their reading of short stories and novels in earlier years is here given a wider perspective as it includes an adult as well. So the novel offers a thematic development for most students.

- *Topics that are relevant to students:*

However, *About a Boy* is not only an educational novel. It touches on a variety of modern issues that teenagers can readily understand. The story probes such diverse issues as the meaning of life, single parenting, the contemporary patchwork family, peer group pressure and the role of pop culture, all of which can lead to lively classroom discussions. One of the reasons why Marcus encounters ridicule and rejection at school is that his mother tries to enforce her particular unconventional views on him instead of letting him either develop his own taste or follow the tastes of his peers. Behind what is on the surface an entertaining novel, the novel contains questions about what constitutes a family in modern Western societies; divorced parents, single parents, extended families and the need for friends all play a role in helping individuals to find their way in a complex society where bonds between individuals and groups have loosened. As Marcus says: 'I feel safer than before ... because I know more people. [...] It doesn't really matter who they are, as long as they are there.'

- *A good read:*

About a Boy is great work of humour that will appeal to students who just wish to read an enjoyable and amusing novel. Reading for fun should never be underestimated, least of all in the language classroom, if we want our students to carry on reading long after their academic education has finished.

- *Straightforward and contemporary language:*

About a Boy is written in a language that is fairly easy to understand, which means it can be read in any class from the 10th upwards and by a whole range of different types of courses with varying learning abilities. Hornby writes in a deceptively simple style that masks his ability to reproduce spoken English like a true master. Often Hornby is accused of being a lightweight writer, but he has a mastery of language that requires talent and skill.

- *An interesting narrative perspective:*

Most stories that deal with the problems of growing-up are usually narrated from an adolescent's point of view. The narrative perspective of Hornby's novel is made up of a continually changing point of view, as the chapters are told alternately from Marcus's and Will's point of view, thus precluding any rash identification with either of the main characters. Hornby casts the reader in the role of an arbiter who must carefully consider his or her sympathies. Thus the reading process differs markedly from that of traditional stories dealing with growing up and the reader becomes familiar with multi-perspectivism; this strengthens the students' competence in dealing with different forms of narrative designs.

- *Film and novel analyses:*

A further reason why *About a Boy* is suitable for the classroom is the fact that the novel has been turned into a successful film. Watching the film provides the opportunity to examine the transformation of one genre (novel) into another (film) and to assess the extent to which that transformation has been carried out successfully. Moreover, the different endings of the novel and the film make for a lively classroom discussion. Analysing the film also offers the students a chance to learn the necessary vocabulary for film analysis and to train the students' media competence.

- *A variety of teaching approaches:*

How the teacher wishes to deal with the novel depends on his or her class and teaching aims. It can be used for student-centred activities and learning groups or for a more teacher-oriented approach. It can be used with difficult classes that do not enjoy reading, with classes that are attempting a *ganzschrift* for the first time or with classes where groups of students can approach the novel in an independent way and present their findings to the rest of the class.

Synopsis of the Novel

General

About a Boy revolves around the worlds of Will Freeman, who has never worked in his life, and Marcus, who has recently moved with his divorced mother to London.

Will lives off the income from the royalties of a Christmas song his father wrote and which Will deeply dislikes. A superficial man with no job who literally lives from half-hour to half-hour with no emotional ties or social obligations to restrict him, Will values his ability to make decisions based solely on his own immediate impulses. He hates any form of commitment and is not interested in a lasting relationship. When he discovers that single mothers are easy to please but are not really looking for a long-term relationship, he decides to attend a single-parent group meeting in the hope of finding short-term sexual partners. For this purpose he invents a son and an ex-wife.

It is during a single-parent outing that Will meets Marcus, the twelve-year-old son of Fiona. He goes on the outing with his mother's friend Suzie, who Will fancies. Fiona is feeling depressed and therefore decides to stay at home. When they take Marcus home, they find Fiona lying unconscious on the floor, as she has tried to commit suicide.

From that moment on Marcus decides to seek out Will, as he believes that Will might help Fiona (and Marcus) by falling in love with her and making her happy again, while providing Marcus with the emotional security of a family. Marcus soon discovers that Will has neither an ex-wife nor a son and blackmails him into becoming a sort of father-figure. He regularly visits him after school and gradually feels less miserable and awkward. Marcus's mother, who is an esoteric hippy, does not really understand her son's worries. Marcus is bullied by his fellow students for wearing strange clothes, having a terrible haircut, listening to outdated music, singing to himself in public and being generally completely out of touch with modern-day youth culture.

Will turns out to be the perfect teacher for Marcus. He shows him how to dress, what sort of haircut to have and introduces him to the band Nirvana. In short, Will teaches Marcus how to be cooler (or at least, more normal).

Helping Marcus, however, also benefits Will. He stops inventing roles for himself, experiences the joy of genuine affection and develops a sense of responsibility. Just as Marcus becomes less of a geek and grows into a more self-confident boy, so Will symbolically grows into adulthood. For the first time in his life he falls in love, and is willing to cope with difficulties and to face responsibilities.

The novel, which is narrated alternately from Marcus's and Will's perspectives, depicts two parallel worlds which force the reader to see the events and characters from these two differing points of view. It is only towards the end that these two worlds merge, as the two protagonists have changed and 'adopted' character traits of the other: having overcome his awkwardness and lost his literal-mindedness, Marcus has acquired some of Will's coolness. Will, by contrast, has stopped pretending and acquired some of Marcus's seriousness.

Chapter by Chapter

① It is the school summer holidays. Marcus's mum, Fiona, has just split up with her boyfriend. She and Marcus have recently moved to London. He is going to start a new school. Marcus's mum and dad split up when he was eight years old. Marcus worries about his mum being unhappy.

② Will Freeman is 36 and views himself as a cool single man. He compares his life to that of his two friends, John and Christine, who have two children and a chaotic house. Will is not envious; he does not want a family and is convinced that his friends are making themselves unhappy. They used to go out a lot together. John asks Will if he'd like to be the godfather of the new baby, but Will has absolutely no interest.

③ Marcus cannot sleep after his first day at his new school. He does not want to go back the next day because he feels he does not fit in, as his mother has made him do different things from other teenagers. He sometimes sings out loud without realizing, which is noticed and joked about by his classmates, and even the teacher makes a joke about it.

④ Will sees a beautiful woman in a record shop. Two days later he sees her again in a café, but discovers it is a different woman (Angie); he arranges a date with her. She tells him about her two kids and Will is enthusiastic. For the next few weeks he plays 'Will the good guy', and takes part in the kids' lives. After six weeks, he finds that kids get in the way of a relationship, but Angie decides to end the relationship anyway. He realizes, for purely selfish reasons, that relationships with single mothers are ideal for him and sets about being 'Mr Nice Guy', in the hope of having more relationships like this.

⑤ Marcus's mum starts crying in the morning, which is unusual, as she normally only cries in the evenings. Marcus does not know what to say or do, so he goes to school. His two friends from the computer club ignore him and then explain that they do not want to be his friends anymore because they get into trouble with other boys.

⑥ Will is having difficulties finding single mothers to have a relationship with, so he invents a two-year-old son, Ned, and joins a single-parents' group (SPAT), with the aim of meeting women. After a slow start he meets Suzie, who he finds attractive. They talk, and Will is sure that he stands a good chance with her.

⑦ Marcus goes into a newsagent's and is reading a magazine when some boys come in and bully him. At home he finds his mother watching cartoons on TV, although she hates them. He tells her that she does not look after him properly. She tells him about the picnic on Saturday with SPAT – she doesn't want to go, but Suzie, who is an old schoolfriend of hers, will take him. Marcus is not keen. His mother tells him that they do not do each other any good, and Marcus is confused.

⑧ The day of the picnic. After telling Suzie about his ex-girlfriend (Ned's mother) and his son, Will now realizes he is in a difficult situation as he will not be able to invite Suzie back to his flat, and feels caught in his own web of lies. In the car Will sits next to Marcus, who he describes as 'the weird kid', and he explains why he does not have to work – his father wrote a Christmas song many years ago, and Will lives off the royalties from it. Will tries to befriend Marcus, but Marcus shows little interest. Marcus tells Suzie that his mother is unhappy. A conversation between Suzie and Will is interrupted by Marcus saying that he thinks he has killed a duck.

⑨ Marcus threw a sandwich at a duck and it is now floating dead in the pond. When the park-keeper accuses Marcus of killing it, Will backs Marcus up and says it was already dead. Marcus, Suzie and Will drive home. When Suzie drops Marcus off, they all go inside and find that Fiona has tried to commit suicide. However, she is not dead.

⑩ They all go to the hospital. Fiona is kept in overnight and Marcus sleeps at Suzie's house.

⑪ Marcus finds the suicide note from his mum and is just reading it when she returns home from hospital. Marcus realizes that two is not a good number for a family, as there is a danger of being left alone, so he decides he will have to find an addition to the family. Marcus and Fiona watch a video; it is supposed to be a comedy, but in fact is also about suicide. When Marcus switches it off, his mum does not understand why; Marcus is finding it difficult to understand her.

⑫ Will phones Suzie to ask after Fiona, and offers to take Marcus out. His days are boring, and he sees this as an opportunity do something without any commitment. He is trying to find something that a twelve-year-old might like to do, when Marcus phones and announces that if Will wants to take him out, his mum will have to come too. They arrange to meet the following Saturday. Will, determined to keep up the pretence of having a child, buys a car-seat.

⑬ Marcus hopes that he and Fiona will go to live with Will and his son, and in this way, nobody will be left alone if one of them dies. Marcus wants to go to Planet Hollywood because it is expensive, but because there is a long queue, they go to another restaurant. The conversation is rather stilted between Will and Fiona at first, but after a while, Marcus is convinced they will move in together.

⑭ Will does not find Fiona attractive, but decides that he would still like to help them. When he is invited to their house for dinner, he finds that Fiona's seriousness about life makes him uneasy and decides against getting involved with Fiona and Marcus. One afternoon, however, Marcus rings his doorbell. Once inside the flat, he notices immediately that Will does not have a son. He promises not to tell his mother if Will goes out with her. Will tells him to go home.

⑮ Marcus goes to Will's flat more and more regularly. They become friends, but Marcus is still unable to talk to him about his mother.

⑯ One afternoon, some bullies from Marcus's school follow him to Will's flat, throwing sweets at him. Marcus explains to Will that they do not like him because he is different. Will decides to take Marcus shopping for some new shoes to make him stick out less. He is very pleased with his generosity until the next day when the kids steal the shoes from Marcus.

⑰ Marcus's mother is furious when she finds out that Marcus has been visiting Will after school, and that Will has been buying him presents. She takes Marcus to Will's flat and forbids Will from seeing him again. When Marcus tries to explain why he goes there, she does not understand, so he tells her he needs a father, which he knows will make her feel bad.

⑱ Fiona calls Will. They decide to meet the next night for a drink and to discuss Marcus. She tells him not to open the door when Marcus visits.

⑲ Fiona has complained to the school about the theft of Marcus's shoes, although Marcus did not want her to. Marcus is called to the headteacher's office. While he is waiting outside, he talks to Ellie, a famous troublemaker three years older than him. She tells him that the face on her sweatshirt is Kurt Cobain, who she tells Marcus is a footballer.

⑳ Marcus rings Will's doorbell until he finally answers. He asks Will to take him and a friend to watch a football match. After some misunderstanding, Will explains to Marcus that Kurt Cobain is in fact a singer.

㉑ Marcus bumps into Ellie at school and tells her he knows who Kurt Cobain is. He strikes up a friendship with her and asks Will if he can invite her to his flat to listen to music. Will does not think she will be interested.

㉒ Will is invited to Marcus's house for Christmas, but he is not looking forward to being with Fiona. However, there are six of them altogether, and they exchange presents.

㉓ Marcus's father provokes an argument by smoking a joint in front of Marcus. Suzie, who Will has not seen since admitting that he is not a father, pops in, and makes Will feel awkward about his earlier lies.

㉔ Will meets Rachel at a New Year's Eve party. He talks about Marcus, and when she assumes that Marcus is his son, Will does not correct her. At the end of the evening they arrange for their kids to meet.

㉕ At Suzie's New Year's Eve party. Marcus sees Ellie and talks to her about his parents. They see Ellie's mum kissing a man in the garden, and when Ellie shouts at her mum, Marcus is surprised that this sort of thing can happen.

㉖ Will tells Marcus that Rachel thinks that they are father and son. Marcus agrees to meet her. They go to her house and meet her son, Ali, who is much cooler than Marcus. When Ali threatens him, Marcus leaves the house.

㉗ Ali threatened to kill Marcus if Will goes out with Rachel. Marcus goes to the bus stop, where Will catches up with him. When Will explains that Ali is crying and is very sorry, Marcus agrees to go back, and everything is fine. Marcus, Ellie and Zoe go to the newsagent's after school, Marcus is bullied again as he waits outside, and Ellie rescues him. Marcus is very impressed.

㉘ Marcus relates the incident to Will. Will is not so sure that Ellie sees Marcus as a potential boyfriend. Will confesses to Rachel that he does not have a son. She says she did indeed find the fact that he had a son made him more interesting.

㉙ Fiona starts crying again regularly in the mornings, but this time Marcus feels he can talk to Will and Ellie. Will, however, does not want to get involved and Ellie is upset because Kurt Cobain tried to kill himself, and Marcus becomes upset because she says people who attempt suicide will try again. Later she finds him and they talk about his mum.

㉚ Will finds Fiona difficult because unlike Will, who is superficial and does not care about anything, Fiona cares enough to kill herself. He discusses the point of life with Rachel and they go to bed together. Rachel offers to show Will how to talk to Fiona.

㉛ Marcus's father has had an accident at home and wants to see his son. Marcus realizes that his father never normally wants to see him and is angry. Ellie offers to go with him. He does not tell Fiona that Ellie will go with him. On the way to meet Ellie at the station, he sees the newspaper headlines that Kurt Cobain has killed himself. He tries to prevent her from seeing them, but she tells him that she knows already and she is planning to get drunk.

㉜ While Marcus is away, Will, Rachel and Fiona plan to meet for a drink. Rachel (intentionally) does not turn up, and so Will is forced to deal with the tearful Fiona. They go back to her house and find a message on the answering machine from Marcus, who is at the police station.

㉝ Marcus realizes that he does not want Ellie as a girlfriend – he needs someone quieter. On the train they argue about whose life is worse, and Ellie gets out of the train. Marcus follows her and they walk through the town. When Ellie sees a shop with a cardboard cutout of Kurt Cobain in the window, she sees it as an exploitation of his death, so she smashes the window. The police take them to the police station where Marcus's dad and his girlfriend are the first to arrive.

㉞ Will, Fiona and Ellie's mother arrive at the police station. The police have also asked the shop owner to come. She is a young woman, who dresses and looks like Ellie, and is in fact a Kurt Cobain fan. They all go to a restaurant.

㉟ Marcus goes to Cambridge to stay with his father, where they talk about whether Marcus needs a father. Marcus thinks that a father figure is not as important as having lots of people around him. He goes back to London.

㊱ Will is in love with Rachel. He often takes Ali and Marcus, who are now friends, out on Saturdays. Marcus is much more mature now and is still friends with Ellie. Fiona is not sure how to deal with her son, who is now more of a typical teenager and can stand up for himself. Will is proud of him.

Teaching the Novel in the Classroom

Different Methods for Different Classes

About a Boy is a novel that can be read with students from the 10th year upwards. If the teacher decides to read the novel in the 10th or 11th years, the approach put forward in this Teacher's Manual may need supplementing or changing. Even though learner autonomy should still remain one of the primary methodological goals, additional help and guidance by the teacher might be required.

However, as many teachers feel more comfortable approaching the teaching unit in a chronological manner, information is provided on p. 8 as to how teachers can divide the novel into reading units and use and adapt the questions that can be found under the section 'Topics' (cf. pp. 14–30).

Teaching *About a Boy* in the *oberstufe* (especially if the novel is to form part of the *abitur*) involves a variety of targets. Students should develop their reading skills (e.g. extensive reading, and finding and understanding key passages), writing skills (especially for specific purposes such as writing a review, a letter-to-the-editor, etc., which serve to practise their argumentative discourse) and their ability to analyse texts largely on their own. Moreover, they should also be expected to develop their creative skills by, for example, turning a passage of the novel into a screenplay or film script. Other targets could include making use of the Internet to do web quests on the social aspects of the novel (e.g. single parenting, teenage fashion and consumerism), which allows students to develop their media competence as well as their ability to select and evaluate non-fictional texts.

While all of the intentions outlined here should be achieveable in a *leistungskurs*, the teacher will have to decide which skills are necessary for a *grundkurs*. Given the truism that both the performance and competence by students in the *grundkurs* often differ greatly, it is next to impossible to suggest specific novel-based skills. However, it should go without saying that reading skills and writing skills must both be trained and expanded.

A Student-Centred Approach to *About a Boy*

Although the teacher may well choose a chronological approach to the novel, the procedure suggested in this Teacher's Manual, however, is somewhat different. A student-centred pre-reading activity is followed by a teacher-based analysis of the first four chapters, which should ensure that all students have dealt with the same areas before they embark on their own group topics.

Students should then read the remaining chapters by themselves. While reading, they should be encouraged to focus on a given topic (cf. pp. 14 ff.), for which they then become the class expert. They make notes, evaluate parts of the novel, present their findings to the class and moderate a discussion about their topic. Finally, they hand in their findings as part of a term paper. This method allows for a variety of teaching goals. It encourages students to:

- practise their reading skills;
- develop their ability to extract and evaluate information;
- develop their presentation skills;
- discuss their findings with their fellow students;
- develop learner autonomy, as they are responsible for organizing their work, e.g. by allocating areas of responsibility among themselves and keeping minutes of their discussions;
- develop social competence by working together with others;
- develop their own text-based responses;
- defend their own responses and views in front of the class;
- learn from others about aspects they have not examined in detail.

The teacher should nevertheless sit in with each of the groups in order to advise them how to read the novel in a way that results in successful teamwork. Student-based approaches does not exclude intervention by the teacher: it may prove necessary to supplement the findings of a group by referring the students to key passages that have either been overlooked or misread and that are central to an adequate understanding of the topic under scrutiny.

Additionally, it may be necessary to practise scanning passages of the novel with individual groups, making them aware of the need to read for gist rather than to understand everything in detail.

Students often cannot analyse a text properly because they lack the vocabulary needed to go beyond a mere description, so they should be asked to jot down their needs (including the vocabulary they need) at the end of the minutes that each group has to hand in to the teacher after their discussion meeting. In this way the teacher not only knows what each group is doing; he or she can also become aware at an early stage of the difficulties the individual groups are facing and be able to act accordingly. The minutes are then returned to each group in the following lesson together with comments and the lexical items the group asked for.

A major aim of the teaching approach suggested in this Teacher's Manual is the practice of presentation skills (cf. Infosheet 1 on p. 43) and this should be gone over in detail with each group. Students should be familiarized with a general model for oral presentations, which the teacher should work out with each group. During a group's presentation students from other groups should take notes concerning grammatical and lexical mistakes and presentation abilities. Constructive peer assessment should be encouraged, and evaluation by the teacher can be included when necessary.

A Teacher-based Approach to *About a Boy*

If the students have little experience in dealing with a *ganzschrift*, the teacher-based approach that is here restricted to the first four chapters may have to be expanded. The topic-related activities could become the object of group work after the novel has been read, so that learner autonomy and presentation skills are at least practised.

Alternatively, the teacher may wish to approach the novel in a chronological way. In this case, it would be helpful to divide the novel into units, as suggested below. The questions from the section 'Topics' (cf. pp. 14–30) have been divided up according to these units, so that the teacher can easily deal with the various topics within the individual units with the help of while-reading tasks. The questions can refer up to all the information gathered from the novel up to the unit, and can be either used for class discussion or given as homework.

Unit 1: The First Four Chapters (cf. p. 10)
- Analyse Marcus's language and communication strategies. What do you notice? Keep notes as you read the novel.
  (cf. Topic 6, p. 26)

Unit 2: Chapters 4–8
- Describe Marcus's and Fiona's relationship.
  (cf. Topic 4, p. 22)
- Summarize in your own words Marcus's life.
  (cf. Topic 6, p. 26).
- Describe Will's relationships with women he has had affairs with or is interested in.
  (cf. Topic 3, p. 20)

Unit 3: Chapters 8–11
- How does Fiona's suicide attempt change Marcus's attitude towards his mother?
  (cf. Topic 4, p. 22)
- Examine Will's initial attitude towards Marcus.
  (cf. Topic 2, p. 17)

Unit 4: Chapters 12–16
- Describe Will's way of life and explain what it tells us about Will.
  (cf. Topic 1, p. 14)
- Analyse Will's attitude towards other people.
  (cf. Topic 1, p. 14)
- What have we learnt so far about Marcus's situation at school?
  (cf. Topic 5, p. 24)
- In what ways does Fiona's suicide attempt change Marcus's life?
  (Cf. Topic 6, p. 26)
- How does Will's action in Ch. 16 compare with his first attempt to get involved in Marcus's and Fiona's lives?
  (cf. Topic 2, p. 17)

Unit 5: Chapters 17–18:
- Describe Fiona's educational principles as depicted on pp. 111–116. How does the mother–son relationship change here?
  (cf. Topic 4, p. 22)
- Comment on Fiona's educational principles. Do you think she is a good mother?
  (cf. Topic 4, p. 22)
- Show how Marcus's life is transformed by his friendship with Will.
  (cf. Topic 6, p. 26)

Unit 6: Chapters 19–31
- Analyse Ellie's manner of speaking and compare it with Marcus's. What differences can you detect?
  (cf. Topic 6, p. 26)
- How does Marcus's friendship with Ellie start to change his life?
  (cf. Topic 5, p. 24)

After the novel has been read
- Explain how the friendship with Ellie contributes to Marcus's emotional and mental growth.
  (cf. Topic 6, p. 26)
- Why does Marcus finally conclude that Ellie would not be an appropriate girlfriend for him?
  (cf. Topic 5, p. 24)
- Describe the main stages of Will's growing commitment to Marcus. Show how he changes his attitude to Marcus.
  (cf. Topic 2, p. 17)
- In what ways does his relationship with Rachel differ from his previous affairs?
  (cf. Topic 3, p. 20)
- How does Will's attitude towards people and his view of life change?
  (cf. Topic 1, p. 14)
- How has Marcus's language changed towards the end of the novel? What do these changes signify?
  (cf. Topic 6, p. 26)

Getting Started

Pre-reading Activity

One major aim of any pre-reading activity is to make students aware of ideas and themes that are central to the novel that they are going to read. Another purpose of such activities peculiar to foreign language teaching is the opportunity it provides to introduce new lexical fields which the student will need in order to cope adequately with the novel.

Worksheet 1: As a pre-reading activity for the whole class, an excerpt can be given to the whole class (cf. p. 45). This particular excerpt introduces the students to Will, one of the two major characters of the novel, and allows them to make predictions as to what might happen in the novel. Of course, one can ask what the title of the novel *About a Boy* might mean, but as an infinite number of answers are possible, with many of them having probably nothing to do with what the novel is in actual fact about, this might not be a productive pre-reading activity. A short excerpt is usually more useful because it helps the students avoid wild speculations, and makes them think about central aspects of the character's life and express themselves with vocabulary that is relevant to the novel.

The responses should be collected either on a transparency or they can be put on a large piece of paper and hung up in the classroom, so that they will remain accessible while the novel is being read.

This excerpt is from the novel you are going to read. Read it carefully. Then jot down your spontaneous ideas on the following:

1. *What do you make of Will?*
2. *What might his life be like?*
3. *What do you expect the novel to be about?*

The first question could yield responses like the following:

- bored, sees no meaning in his life, dissatisfied with his life
- unemployed, doesn't know what to do with his life
- lives only for the moment, is not future-orientated, has no plans
- very self-centred, only cares about himself
- afraid of taking responsibilities
- strange person

The second question could elicit the following responses, which extend the notions above so that the students' perceptions of Will are not only reinforced but also take on a specific shape:

- lonely, unexciting and uneventful
- seems unable to develop visions
- seems to have no close friends
- 'enriches' his life by inventing things.

The students are now in the position of being able to make tentative guesses as to the subject of the novel (third question):

- about a man who is single, falls in love with a woman who has a boy; he changes his way of life and becomes a responsible stepfather;
- about the changes in Will's life, how he finds a meaning in his life;
- about Will's confused life and how he manages to change it.

Taken together, the responses to the question should have made the students aware of major character traits of one of the protagonists, given them the idea that in some way the novel will be about changes in Will's life and thus aroused their curiosity as to what *About a Boy* is really about.

Getting into the Novel:
Guided Analysis of Chapters 1–4

The students are then asked to read the first four chapters. Classroom discussion of these chapters should be teacher-based. The aim is to work out major textual features (character analysis, narrative mode, aspects of language, etc.) so that the students will have a frame of orientation for their topic-related activities. The following questions might help make the student aware of the various textual features. It is probably worthwhile reading the first two chapters in class. The students should also be encouraged to ask about any words they do not understand.

Some teachers, especially those whose students are reading a novel for the first time in class, may also want to refer to Chapter Three of *English Eleven 2000* (Cornelsen, Berlin, 2000; Best.-Nr. 358160), which offers an interesting student-based approach to novel-reading for students unused to reading a complete and original novel in a foreign language. One of the novels used in Chapter Three is *About a Boy*.

Chapter One

1. *What is the reader immediately confronted with?*

There is no introduction/exposition of any kind. The reader is immediately confronted with a dramatic family situation: the separation of two adults.

2. *How is that event narrated?*

The narration is third person, but it is from the limited point of view of twelve-year-old Marcus, so the narrative mode is that of selective ommiscience.

3. *How does Marcus deal with the situation?*

He reacts in an unusual way: he is very calm and reasonable, almost to the point of being pragmatic.

4. *Analyse the dialogue between Marcus and his mother. What does it tell us about their relationship?*

Mother and son are very close, they talk to each other as if they were on equal terms. Yet on closer analysis, Fiona seems to be childish, even unreasonable; Marcus, by contrast, seems to be more mature than his age would suggest. One might speculate that a certain reversal of roles has taken place, although the reader is aware of the limitations of the point of view of a twelve-year-old.

5. *Read this chapter again. What impression does the reader get of Marcus?*

First impressions of Marcus: he is caring and sensitive; he talks like a friend to his mother; he is precocious.

In summary, the students could be asked to state what the chapter focuses on and how it relates to the pre-reading text (cf. p. 45). At this point some speculation about the development of the plot is appropriate.

6. *How do you think the story will continue?*

Chapter Two

1. *Marcus is introduced while confronting a dramatic family situation. How is Will Freeman introduced to the reader?*

Will is introduced in quite a different way. He is filling in a questionnaire that is probably not intended for men over 30, and is reacting in a way that would also seem untypical for someone of his age. His life seems to be well-ordered, unspectacular, marked by routine. He is presented in an amusing way, because the things for which he awards himself points are so trivial.

2. *What is his life like? Jot down your initial impressions.*

First impressions of Will Freeman: he does not seem to take things seriously; he seems immature, like a teenager; he is an idle loafer who does not work; he is single; he lives for today and has no responsibilities

The teacher can then ask the students in groups to do the two following tasks, with half the class doing one of the tasks and the other half the other.

3. *Compare the two first chapters in which the reader is introduced to Marcus and Will. What differences do you notice and how is the effect created?*

Will seems to be the opposite of Marcus because he is immature. Will is egocentric, self-centred, while Marcus is caring. The different introductions give an idea of the kind of person both are, but the reader has the feeling that there is a role reversal, with the young boy being mature and the older man being immature. Marcus is introduced through a dialogue with his mother, which then leads to his thoughts about their life and his worries about his mother. Will is introduced reading a glossy magazine, and is then seen rejecting family life and emotional ties.

4. *Look at the pre-reading excerpt and the second chapter. Would you say that Will's character has developed between the first chapter and the excerpt, or is he basically the same person?*

By and large, he is the same person. He cannot see himself as a father taking responsibility for children, which reinforces the fact that he is immature. One can see that in both excerpts he fills his time with trivial things, and that he is shallow (and proud of it).

After this has been done, the teacher can then start to ask for links between the two chapters and bring in the question of the title of the novel:

5. *What has Will Freeman got to do with Marcus and his mother?*

6. *Who do you think the 'Boy' in the title* About a Boy *is? Who will the story be about?*

Chapter Three

1. *How does Marcus see himself?*

He sees himself as shy, he feels uncomfortable among his peers and misplaced at school.

2. *What is his situation at school like?*

He is ridiculed because he is different; he is considered a weakling and an eccentric; he feels unfairly treated by his English teacher.

3. *Why do other people think that Marcus is weird?*

He sometimes sings aloud in class and daydreams during lessons. He is a loner, withdrawn and undemanding.

4. *Go through Chapter Three again and jot down words and phrases that could be used to describe Marcus and then do a brief character description of him.*

Quotes: pp. 14–15: 'horrible feeling' (l. 9), 'He'd still be who he was, and that ...was the basic problem' (ll. 14–15), 'He just wasn't right for schools' (l. 16), 'he wasn't right for parties, because he was too shy' (ll. 18–19), 'he hated standing up in front of people' (ll. 35–36); pp. 16–17: 'he was usually wearing the wrong shoes or the wrong trousers, and his haircut was wrong all the time' (ll. 11–13), 'Marcus knew he was weird' (l. 15), 'reading books ... made him different' (ll. 42–43), 'he could feel himself floating away from everyone and everything' (ll. 45–46), 'the tune just sort of slipped out' (ll. 50–51); p. 18: 'he could see really clearly ... what was going to happen' (ll. 1–3), 'He knew what she was doing and why' (l. 26).

Marcus: an initial description:

He is shy, withdrawn, afraid of his peers; he is not trendy, not up to date with pop culture; he suffers from low self-esteem; he is very sensitive and perceptive; he doesn't feel understood by his teachers; he never had a 'real' childhood; he is aware of his problems.

Chapter Four

1. *Analyse and evaluate Will's attitude towards women.*

He treats women like objects, he does not want a lasting relationship and has no desire to have a family. He does not want to make any compromises or change his lifestyle because of a woman. He cannot commit himself emotionally and so exploits women emotionally. He might be called a predator.

2. *How does Will see himself?*

He sees himself as the perfect lover for single women, he thinks he is loved not for what he is but for what he appears to be. He considers himself to be a good actor and role player, as a man without depth or substance. All in all he is self-satisfied and not at all self-critical.

3. *What would you consider to be his most striking characteristic?*

Students might mention one of the following: egocentric, cynical, lacking responsibility, self-satisfied, self-contented, deceptive.

4. *What is my attitude towards Will and Marcus? Why do I have this attitude?*

The task is demanding as it involves reflection on the reading process. Ideally, selected student responses to Will and Marcus may be used as a starting point for a discussion.

The result on p. 12 may be put on the blackboard:

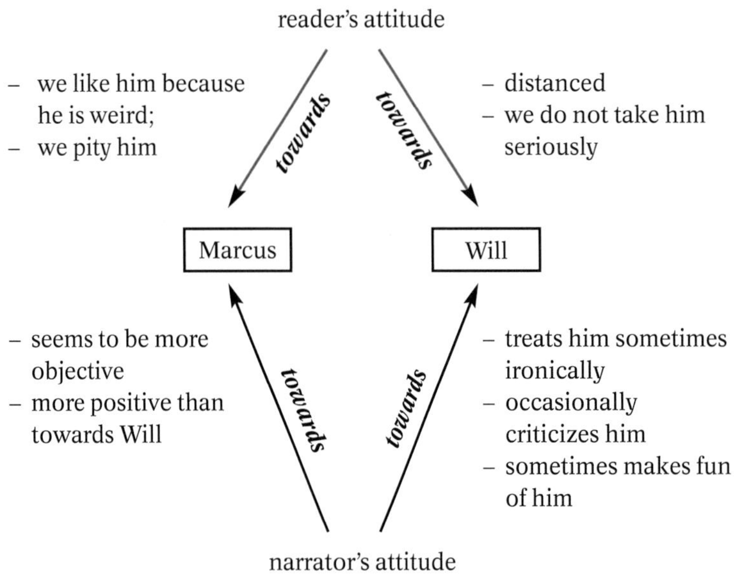

Character Profiles

Once the first four chapters have been read, the teacher can hand out Worksheets 2 and 3 (cf. pp. 46 and 47), so that the students can gather their initial impressions of Marcus and Will before embarking on their chosen topics and reading the rest of the novel. Possible answers:

Worksheet 2:
Facts about his life: Marcus is 12 years old; he lives with his mum; they have moved from Cambridge to London; his parents are divorced; he has started a new school.
Relationships with others: open, talkative relationship with his mum; they discuss their problems openly; he tries to cheer his mother up (but his mum does not seem to take his problems seriously, e. g. about school: 'you'll get used to it'); no friends at school, so he feels isolated; ridiculed by others.
Characteristics: self-aware; perceptive; sensitive; caring; nervous; shy; tolerant; lonely; precocious; not trendy.
Problems: school; his mother's relationships and general sadness.
Examples of his language: 'Have you split up now?' (asks many questions); 'It looks to be like you've split up. But I just wanted to make sure' (inquisitive); 'Or we could pick the pepperoni off' (worries about minor things); 'More happened, and that had to be a good thing' (rational)

Worksheet 3:
Facts about his life: 36 years old; reads trivial magazines; has taken drugs; goes clubbing; earns a lot of money for doing nothing.
Relationships: dislikes children; wants friends for entertainment value; avoids emotional commitment; uninterested in others.
Characteristics: egocentric; immature; lazy; cynical; lacking responsibility; self-satisfied; self-contented; deceptive, role-playing.
Problems: His image and how to maintain it; other people and their problems; people wanting commitment; getting easy, casual sex.
Examples of his use of language: 'He was sub-zero! He was dry ice! He wasFrosty the Snowman! He would die of hypothermia' (amusing but trivial); 'you didn't have to have a life of you own any more' (honest); 'Been burning the candle at both ends?' (unaware of others); 'People who looked like Julie Christie' (gives roles to others); 'I would have been disappointed if you didn't have children' (lying to win people over); 'Will the Good Guy, Will the Redeemer' (role-playing); 'he could walk hand-in-hand with a beautiful woman, children gambolling happily in front of him, and everybody could see him doing it' (image important).

Reading Log

Once the students have read these four chapters extensively, it would be an appropriate time to ask them to start keeping a reading log. This will be particularly useful for 10- and 11th-year students, but could also be used by students in other years, especially by those who may wish to refer back to the novel if it forms part of their *abitur*.

Should the students have no experience with reading logs, they could discuss in class what a reading log should look like and what its purpose is.

For many a reading log will simply be a good reminder of how the story develops, so that if the teacher wishes to set a *klassenarbeit*, they will be able to revise more effectively. As *About a Boy* is quite a long novel, this will be seen to be a sensible idea in the long run.

A basic reading log for the first two chapters should contain answers to the classical wh-questions: Who? Where? When? What? But there should be space for comments, etc.

Chapter	Who	Where	When	What	Comments

A reading log should contain not only information of the type described above, but also separate sections on:

- *Character development.* Students should keep a record of such items of information that they consider important for their personal understanding of Will and Marcus (e.g. state of mind, character development) or of other characters in the novel. This could either be done as a separate column next to the chronological table of events, so that the different types of information can be related (with arrows or color markings), or students could start an extra 'comments' page, on which they note such items of information, as well as open questions (and perhaps later, the answers).
- *Aspects of language.* Anything concerning vocabulary could be kept here, e.g. words the students would like to learn and use actively, collocations that occur frequently, language that reflects on the characters.
- *Quotations.* It is always useful for later reference if students jot down quotations they think shed light on the characters or the ideas in the novel. They should include page and line references.
- *Information about the topics in the novel.* This will be especially true if the class follows the student-based approach as suggested in this Teacher's Manual.
- *Extra material.* Students could say how the novel relates to other novels they have read, or films they have seen; they could include references to music, films, etc. in the novel. It is definitely possible to enjoy the novel without taking specific notice of these references – as a matter of fact, it is quite likely that most of the young readers who read the book in Britain will not be familiar with a lot of them. Nonetheless they offer an opportunity for students to become acquainted with other forms of entertainment and to do individual research on specific areas (e.g. pop music should provide an incentive to many) that interests them. More information on the 'trivia' mentioned in *About a Boy* can be found at www.learnetix.de/bookshelf · About a Boy.
- *The individual student's personal evaluation of the reading process* (the novel itself and how it is dealt with in class).

Students should be invited to share their reading experiences in groups during the English lesson, and accordingly write parts of their notes in class after or during such group sessions.

For a lengthy description of a reading log, the students could download the document at: www.learnetix.de/bookshelf • Skills • Lesen. Here they can find a detailed description of things they might like to keep in their reading log.

Topics

Here is a list of topics related to the novel. In order to encourage learner autonomy, the students should be told to pick one of them and then write notes about it while reading the novel. Once they have finished reading the novel, the students should then give a short presentation to the class of their topic. Infosheet 1 on p. 42 offers some advice as to how work can be organized. The teacher san supplement his or her own topics if he or she feels other aspects should be looked at.

1. **Will Freeman: his way of life and his attitudes towards people**
2. **Will's changing attitude towards Marcus**
3. **Will's relationships with women**
4. **Marcus and Fiona: the mother–son relationship**
5. **Marcus' situation at school and his friendship with Ellie**
6. **The stages of Marcus's development**
7. **Marcus: an analysis of his language**

On the following pages there are questions that the teacher may give more inexperienced students. These questions are intended to guide the students while reading the novel and making notes on their selected topic.

Should the teacher prefer the class to be more teacher-oriented, he or she can use these questions as the basis for classroom discussion. Either way, there are suggested answers and helpful tables and graphs, which the teacher may decide to use as he or she sees fit. Page references are also given. If the teacher is working through the novel chronologically, this does require more work, as the topics and questions will need to be integrated into the teaching process at the appropriate time (cf. p. 8).

As some of the topics overlap, the student-centred approach makes sense, because students from other groups will be able to contribute actively to the presentations on other topics.

1. Will Freeman: His Way of Life and His Attitude Towards People

If the class is reading the novel together with the teacher playing a more active role, it would be best to give the class Questions 1–3 before Ch. 16, as this is when Will starts to show more disinterested feelings towards a fellow human being (i.e. Marcus). Question 3 is basically a summary of what the students have learned about Will's character. The questions should ideally be given out before the students have read too much, so that they can collect information and quotes while reading. Question 4 can only be answered once the whole novel has been read.

1. *Describe Will's way of life and explain what it tells us about Will.*

From the work on Ch. 2 and 4, students should already have formed an opinion of Will Freeman as being a person who is more at home in the world of trivia than in the world of real people.

Idleness: His life is marked by inertia; it is an endless repetition of trivial daily chores that lack significance.

- Trivia: In Ch. 2 he fills in a magazine questionnaire and considers the result 'as close as he had ever come to an achievement' (p. 10, ll. 5–6). He uses magazines, TV and music to get through the day (p. 10, ll. 20–24). Shopping, sport, friends and books help for the rest of the time (p. 87, ll. 66–69).
- Getting through the day: He divides the day into units of time to get by (p. 69, ll. 50ff.).
- Work: He has never worked and never had to work as he lives off the royalties from his father's Christmas song. More importantly, he does not really want to work (p. 48, ll. 23–29). Occasionally he sends off letters of application with a half-filled CV, but has never been offered anything (p. 70, ll. 12–27).
- Voluntary work: Occasionally he thinks of doing altruistic work, e.g. working in a soup kitchen, but he never gets further than the organizational step (p. 34, ll. 15–19).

Role-playing: Noticeable is the way he creates roles for himself and for those around him:

- 'Uncle Will' (p. 21, l. 63): When he discovers that Angie has a child, he envisions himself as possibly being 'good with children, even though he hated them' (p. 21, ll. 60–61). He plays the role well, but children have a tendency to ruin the good things in life (p. 24, ll. 13–23).
- 'Will the Good Guy, Will the Redeemer' (p. 22, l. 25): He brings joy into Angie's life, which makes him feel as though he is superhuman.
- 'serial nice guy' (p. 26, l. 18): This follows on from his affair with Angie. Married women offer him the ability to have short flings during which he can hide his superficial persona. This gets him involved in SPAT (Ch. 6).
- 'single father' (p. 33, l. 9): The biggest deception he plays is his lie about being a single father so that he can join SPAT and meet single mothers.
- 'Robert de Niro' (p. 38, l. 29): He invents a strong emotional act when discussing his imaginary wife and child.
- C.S. Lewis (p. 46, l. 4): He invents a fantasy world to impress a schoolfriend, and almost ends up believing it himself.
- Angie becomes Julie Christie (p. 22, l. 6): It is as if the real Angie is not interesting enough, but when she becomes a celebrity, he can relate to her.

He invents roles for himself and those around him. But his imaginary roles and situations are usually someone else's. It is as though Will views life as an ongoing film in which he plays various roles as the situation requires. Most of the roles are not particularly imaginative and he is let down by his inability to complete the imaginary storyline successfully (p. 45, ll. 32–49).

Conclusion: There is no real purpose to his life. He is an onlooker on life, an observant bystander who distances himself from any involvement in life around him. This way of life has entailed a retreat from reality into the substitute world of soaps and pop; moreover, when he does engage with the outside world it is in the form of role-playing. However it must be emphasized that it is a lifestyle he enjoys and feels comfortable with – it is one he has chosen and it fits well with his character.

2. *Analyse Will's attitude towards other people.*

Friendship: Will sees people as being useful only to the degree that they can offer him something (e.g. going clubbing with him, p. 12, ll. 24–26) and relates to them accordingly. Once his friends settle down, he has no more use for them (p. 12, ll. 35–39). His acquaintances have been picked up at social events, e.g. at sports, the pub, etc. (p. 69, ll. 40–42) and they all exist to help him pass the time successfully (p. 69, ll. 45–46). Real friendship involves dealing with the ups and downs that people go through; Will is only interested in the ups (or at least the social aspects of friendship). Other people's emotions and sincerity only serve to bother him.

Relationships: Will seems to have a series of meaningless relationships:

- Jessica (p. 12, ll. 24–35) was a person who he merely wanted to go clubbing with. When she wants a more substantial relationship, Will drops her.

- Angie (p. 22, ll. 1–24) is very attractive, so he re-creates himself in the role of the man she is looking for (caring, sympathetic and interested in children).
- Single mothers: As they seem so grateful to find a man who will accept them with their children but yet are actually not really looking for a relationship, Will decides to start looking for 'temporary parenthood' (p. 26, l. 14).
- By and large, Will is looking for meaningless flings which do not last for a long time. Hence his 'poor romantic track record' (p. 34, ll. 7–8). Love is a way of losing control over one's own life (p. 159, ll. 44–52).

Children: Children require attention, something that would distract Will from his self-centred existence. They create a mess and make people tired and less fun. He seems to have no interest whatsoever in them (p. 11, ll. 39–50, 54–67; p. 12, ll. 1–23, 29–35).

He only becomes interested in children when he thinks it is a good way of meeting women (p. 21, ll. 64–67), and even convinces himself that he would be good with children.

When he does start hanging around with Angie's children, it is not a very deep relationship because it is largely about his self-image ('photo-opportunity', p. 22, l. 38; 'everyone could see him doing it', p. 23, l. 41). And afterwards he is able to retire back into his sheltered world (p. 23, ll. 41–42).

In the end, children make relationships dull, as they continually get in the way (p. 24, 13–23).

3. *What is Will's attitude to life?*

- He avoids any commitments or obligations to anyone or anything. Because he has no responsibilities he has become an aimless person who is drifting along.
- Never having been faced with any challenges, he has not discovered anything about his own capabilities.
- He sees people as being useful only to the degree that they can offer him something and relates to them accordingly.
- He has no opinions about anything other than his own well-being and the world of popular culture in which he has immersed himself.
- His life is basically a hedonistic, sheltered and artificial affair; he is utterly self-centred and egocentric and lacks any genuine feelings. All in all, his existence is similar to that of a child who has not yet experienced any hardships or misery in life.
- Yet, basically, Will enjoys his carefree lifestyle and seems to have no difficulty living as he does.

4. *How does Will's attitude towards people and his view of life change?*

Two things happen more or less at the same time that alter his view of life:
- **Marcus** enters into Will's life. For the first time Will starts to develop an interest in another person's life and begins to be concerned about another person's well-being. Interestingly it is precisely Will's juvenile nature that allows him to help Marcus (p. 138, ll. 10–20).
- **Love:** He falls in love with Rachel (p. 159). He begins to review the kind of existence he has led so far; he stops his role-playing and pretending and starts to confront hardships.

The changes he undergoes are as follows:
- To his own surprise he discovers that this gives him pleasure (p. 106, ll. 38–47).
- He starts to feel affection for someone from whom he does not really need anything (p. 107, l. 47; p. 189, ll. 38–40: p. 193, ll. 58–61).
- He worries about people and becomes aware that he cares about other people (p. 225, ll. 57–62; p. 234, ll. 25–41).
- He tries to be honest (p. 189, 50–56) because he views Rachel as being someone with whom he would like to have a long-term relationship.
- Falling in love makes him want to have an identity which he can offer someone else (p. 193, ll. 62–67).

A third event occurs that helps him acknowledge the fact that he cannot live a sheltered existence:
- **Listening/Talking:** Rachel furtively gets him to talk one-to-one with Fiona about her problems (p. 209, ll. 45–58; pp. 219ff.) without Will realizing he is being set up. Despite initial difficulties worrying about how to talk to Fiona, Will discovers it is not too complicated to listen to someone in an altruistic way (p. 223, l. 71 – p. 224, l. 32).
  It is interesting to note that his relationship with Marcus is what makes him start to listen. On pp. 121–126 the reader is shown the first example of Will talking to someone because of his relationship with (and affection for) Marcus: he has a long conversation with Fiona about Marcus ('He listened to what she said, he thought about it, he answered. He couldn't remember the last time that had happened.' p. 122, ll. 30–31).
  Marcus is the catalyst that gets him involved in other people; through him he can talk to others and even fall in love.

Conclusion: Caring about people makes life messier and more difficult to control but it makes an individual more human (p. 242, ll. 2–9) – and more vulnerable (p. 253, ll. 56–57).

2. Will's Changing Attitude Towards Marcus

Will's attitude changes over the course of the novel. It is a gradual change and is deftly handled by the author. Therefore it is important to divide this topic into three sections (as is suggested by the three questions): a) initial impressions, b) turning point, c) character change. The third question encompasses all three sections. The chart on p. 19 may be given to the class after this topic has been dealt with.

1. *Examine Chapter Eight and Ten in detail and determine Will's initial attitude towards Marcus.*

Chapter Eight: Here Will and Marcus meet for the first time while attending the SPAT picnic with Suzie and her infant daughter Megan, but they have little to do with each other; Will is trying to chat up Suzie, while Marcus is tagging along because his mother feels depressed and wants to be alone.

Will's first impressions of Marcus:

- 'the strange kid' (p. 44, l. 6), 'the weird kid' (p. 44, l. 26; p. 47, l. 44).
- Marcus makes strange noises ('humming tunelessly', p. 46, l. 26) and strange comments ('Michael Jackson ... makes a million pounds a minute', p. 47, ll. 43–44).
- Marcus does not fit the image he has of a teenager (p. 48, ll. 35–38).
- He seems older than his age (p. 50, ll. 18–22).
- He is 'merciless' when he finds a person's vulnerability (p. 50, ll. 27–28).

Will tries to use Marcus to impress Suzie:

- 'it wouldn't do him any harm with Suzie if he were to strike up a sparky, mutually curious relationship with her friend's son' (p. 49, ll. 41–43).

His attempts to win over Marcus fail:

- Marcus is not interested in football (p. 49, l. 46) or hip-hop (p. 49, l. 57).
- Marcus seems to make fun of him by asking him if he gets his questions from a book and telling him that only old people listen to what Will thinks is trendy music.

Conclusion: Will's first impressions of Marcus are unfavourable. When Marcus then fails to respond as Will expects, Will goes on the defensive. Having failed to win him over, he then avoids him just as he does the other adults.

Chapter Ten: Will accompanies Suzie and Marcus to the hospital. This is obviously, objectively seen, a dramatic event, as Fiona has just tried to commit suicide. Will has witnessed Marcus's emotionally most distressing experience.

Will starts to notice more about Marcus:

- 'the boy was probably quite bright' (p. 59, l. 27), as he is aware of what his mother's suicide means. Will might have noticed that Marcus was bright earlier at the picnic (after all, he deflated Will's ego and was both aware of and honest about his mother's depression), but Will was only really interested in Marcus as a teenage boy and in his status as an object through whom he could impress Suzie.

However, Will is not interested in Marcus or his family as people, only in the drama itself:

- 'a really good disease-of-the-week film' (p. 60, l. 3).
- 'However absorbing he was finding the evening's entertainment, he certainly didn't intend to repeat it: this lot were too weird' (p. 60, ll. 8–10).
- 'It had all been very interesting, but he wouldn't want to do it every night' (p. 62, ll. 10–11).

Conclusion: Will sees Marcus's problems as being little more than entertainment. As the reader already knows that Will lives in a make-believe world of films, etc. (cf. p. 15 of the TM), it does not come as a great surprise that this dramatic and emotional event has been reduced to a TV movie one can switch off.

2. *Which incident prompts Will to become actively involved in Marcus's life? Compare it to Will's first attempt to get involved in Marcus's and Fiona's life.*

Ch. 16 is the turning point in the relationship between Will and Marcus, as it is here that Will starts to take an altruistic interest in Marcus.

In Ch. 12–14 Will does show an interest in Marcus and Fiona, but this can be linked to his attempts to do voluntary work (p. 34, ll. 15–21). It is a half-hearted attempt to do something for other people so he can feel good about himself. Will is really more interested in his carefree lifestyle.

However, Marcus, who is craving help and support, begins to force himself into Will's life and visits Will regularly after school. The main reason for these visits is Marcus's fear of going back home and discovering his mother has yet again attempted to kill herself. Marcus's presence gradually changes Will's life, as Will, more or less in spite of himself, is drawn into the boy's worries and needs.

Although Marcus turns up regularly at his place, Will does not really find out much about Marcus and his problems. Being superficial means not delving into other people's problems, so he only touches on Marcus's differences (e.g. talking about getting a new haircut, p. 94, ll. 29–53). It is only when he discovers that Marcus is being bullied on his doorstep that Will becomes really aware of Marcus's problems and takes the initiative.

And it is here that Will's character triumphs. It is due to the fact that Will is a fashion-conscious pseudo-teenager that he, more than the responsible intelligent adults around Marcus (e.g. Suzie or Marcus's teachers), realizes that Marcus's uncool outward appearance has led him to become an object of ridicule among his fellow pupils. As he puts it to Marcus: 'How about if you wear the same clothes and haircut and glasses as everyone else?' (p. 104, ll. 31–32). So he takes Marcus to buy him a pair of trendy and expensive Adidas trainers. The effect of this purchase is even greater on Will than it is on Marcus. For the first time in his life Will has done something purely for altruistic reasons and he experiences a hitherto unknown feeling of self-esteem. From this point onwards he becomes truly involved in Marcus's life. But a character change does take time and it would be wrong to see Will as a completely different person merely for having performed one 'good' deed.

3. *Describe the main stages of Will's growing commitment to Marcus. Show how he changes his attitude to Marcus.*

If the teacher wishes to give the students a little help, he or she could give the group or class the six bold headings (or adapt them) in the answer – 'initial impressions', 'a helping hand', 'companionship', 'involvement', 'commitment' and 'affection' – so that the students can examine the slow but gradual change in Will's relationship with Marcus.

Initial impressions: Will is not stupid and although his immediate impressions are of the appearance and strange manner of the youngster, he nevertheless is aware of Marcus's strengths.
A helping hand: Will even makes a half-hearted attempt to help the boy by taking him (and his mother) out. However, he is Will and Will is not really interested in other people's lives, so this strategy is doomed to failure.
Companionship: Marcus starts to turn up at Will's flat. For a while, Will is in two minds about his relationship with Marcus. On the one hand, he feels genuine affection for the boy, on the other hand he would prefer to sustain his fondness for him by keeping Marcus and his problems at a distance. He talks to Marcus about being different, but no action is forthcoming. Will is merely a shelter from Marcus's home problems.
Involvement: This unusual companionship gives way to a genuine involvement when Will realizes that Marcus is being bullied at school for being different. To help him stick out less Will buys Marcus a pair of trainers. It is the first real action that Will has taken to help someone else. Fiona recognizes Will's new role ('you're involved now', p. 125, l. 67). But Will is still not convinced (p. 126, ll. 12–13; pp. 134, ll. 1–23).
Commitment: It is only when Will wakes up to the fact that Marcus needs help to be a teenager and that Will is perfectly qualified to provide that kind of assistance that a form of commitment emerges. Will is able to give Marcus the advice that a teenager needs to get through these difficult years (p. 138, ll. 10–20).
Affection: Will's acquaintanceship with Marcus allows him to get to know him better. He becomes aware of his good nature (p. 151, ll. 57ff.; p. 189, ll. 38–40) and feels affection for him, just as Marcus feels affection for Will; he worries about him too (p. 225, ll. 57–60). This is even evident to outsiders like Rachel (p. 193, ll. 59–60; p. 206, ll. 12–22).

At the end Will takes not only Marcus but also Ali out for afternoon treats. So the affection he feels for Marcus continues, even though he does feel slightly sad that Marcus has changed from being a weird yet special individual to being a more normal teenager and that the sincere, good, vulnerable and innocent Marcus seems to be disappearing (p. 250, ll. 32–37); from this the reader can appreciate that even at the beginning of the story Will could appreciate the goodness of Marcus – a goodness which Will himself so clearly lacked.
Conclusion: Will's growing commitment to Marcus has a profound effect on his own outlook on life. It is by being with Marcus that Will discovers the importance of sincerity, of getting involved, of helping people and looking after them. And it is through Marcus that Will becomes aware of the fact that whereas previously 'he had never had any kind of intuition or empathy or connection in his life before, ... he had it now' (p. 225, ll. 57–58). Will, who had initially prided himself on being 'super cool', has shed his skin (p. 253, l. 53), become vulnerable and, at the same time, grown up emotionally. His involvement with Marcus has thus transformed him into a responsible, mature and sincere adult.

Will's changing attitude towards Marcus

Initially	**Later**	**Finally**
Thinks Marcus (and his family) are weird. Sees Marcus as part of his 'good works' charitable goal. Lonely Marcus thrusts himself on Will, seeks his help Will wants to keep his distance. Against his will he is drawn into the boy's worries and needs	First act of involvement: he buys trainers for Marcus. Discovers his ability to help Marcus. He turns Marcus into his 'son'. He spends Christmas with him and his family.	Starts to notice Marcus's good nature. He worries about him. He takes Marcus (and Ali) out for treats. He misses the 'old Marcus'.
Involuntary, temporary involvement →	Voluntary act of involvement →	Genuine affection

Transformation of Will

Coolness, distance → Self-centred superficiality	Concern → Discovery of self-esteem	genuine, unconditional commitment Discovery of empathy and sincerity Symbolic rebirth
No commitment to anyone or anything	Participating in life	Discovery of his own humanity

3. Will's Relationships with Women

Students dealing with this topic should concentrate on the affairs Will has at the beginning (up to p. 26), his attempted fling with Suzie (Ch. 6 and 8) and finally his meeting with Rachel in Ch. 24.

1. *What were Will's relationships with his previous partners like? Consider in particular his affair with Jessica.*

Relationships: Will has a series of meaningless relationships:

- Jessica (p. 12, ll. 24–35) was a person who he merely wanted to go clubbing with. When she wanted a more substantial relationship, Will dropped her. Jessica wanted more from life than the 'froth and frivolity'; she wanted to settle down and have a family.
- Angie (p. 22, ll. 1–24) is very attractive, so he recreates himself in the role of the man she is looking for (caring, sympathetic and interested in children). He is almost relieved when she breaks off the relationship, as he was getting tired of her (pp. 24–25).
- Suzie (Ch. 6 and 8) is a single mother. Will tries to engratiate himself with her, but does not get very far, as Marcus intervenes when he kills the duck and then Fiona attempts suicide. Moreover, Will has lied about having a son, which one day Suzie will find out about if they have a relationship.

Conclusion: Will is used to having relationships that leave him free from any obligations. As he is not family-minded, he has no interest in forming a lasting relationship. As Will does not know what love is, he has no intention whatsoever of becoming committed in any way.

2. *In what way does his relationship with Rachel differ from his previous affairs?*

Will had never really fallen in love – indeed never wanted to fall in love – before he met Rachel (p. 159). He just wanted to have sex and had never had serious intentions or plans for the future with other women (p. 12, ll. 24–25, p. 26, ll. 9–18; p. 122, ll. 13–18).

He meets Rachel on New Year's Eve, and is immediately struck by her.

Will's impression of Rachel:

- 'nervy, glamorous, Bohemian, clever, lots of long unruly hair' (p. 159, ll. 41–42), 'intelligent, cultured, ambitious, beautiful, witty' (p. 160, l. 4)
- She is his 'computer-generated ideal life-partner' (p. 159, l. 54).

The reader only gets a vague idea as to why Will reacts differently to her. Angie was exceptionally attractive, but she did not have this effect on him. There are two ways of understanding the effect:
a) the answer 'I dunno' (p. 164, ll. 16–23), which is the reason giving for splitting up (and is therefore somewhat akin to getting together);
b) Will's relationship with Marcus has made him more open to human emotions.
The author, however, does not give any hint as to why Rachel has this effect on Will.

Will's self-awareness:

- 'he couldn't see anything he might have which could interest her' (p. 159, ll. 57–58).
- He feels like a 'blank twit, a cypher, someone who has done nothing all his life' (p. 160, ll. 5–6).
- 'at his core he was ugly and monosyllabic' (p. 160, ll. 18–19).
- 'he was the only person in the room who neither moved nor shook' (p. 161, ll. 56–57).
- 'The most interesting thing about his life ... was Marcus' (p. 162, ll. 11–12).

Will's reaction to Rachel:

- He tells a white lie by implying that Marcus is his son (p. 162, ll. 23ff.). In the past it was not unusual for him to lie to women in order to get their interest. In this case it is the first time that he does not want to lie to a woman, but, having established he is uninteresting, there seems no other possibility of making Rachel interested in him.
  Will had previously invented a similar lie, when he pretended to be a single father with a two-year-old son, Ned, just to go to the SPAT meetings and meet attractive single mothers (pp. 33–38). But this time it is not such an obvious lie, because he never actually says that Marcus was his son. However, Rachel naturally presumes that Marcus is his son and initially Will does nothing to contradict her.
- He is not able to maintain this lie to Rachel. He is afraid that he might lose her if she finds out that he lied, and he tries in his own way to be honest (pp. 189–193). It is the first time that it is really important to him to be honest to a woman.
- Will wants Rachel to be his girlfriend. 'He wanted Rachel to be his wife, his lover, the centre of his whole world; a girlfriend implied that he would see her from time to time, that she would have some kind of independent existence away from him, and he didn't want that at all' (p. 174, ll. 30–33). For the first time Will sees himself in terms of someone else, no longer as a self-sufficient isolated person.
- His interest in Rachel is so strong that he would give everything to be with her and it does not even matter to him if they have sex or not (p. 176, ll. 30–34; p. 204, ll. 12–20).

Rachel's influence:

- Rachel herself takes the initiative once. She gets Will to talk to Fiona, by saying she will meet Will and Fiona, but she herself does not turn up. Will is therefore forced to listen to Fiona's problems and talk to her about them (p. 219–224). Rachel is smart enough to see that Will feels intimidated by the thought of talking about emotional problems to Fiona, so she sets him up (p. 234, ll. 7–15).

Conclusion: Whereas he previously treated women as sex objects – one might even say that he consumed them – now everything has changed. Although it frightens him to want Rachel so much, to feel so vulnerable by loving another person (since she might at any time decide that he was too much trouble), he knows that it is worth taking the trouble with Rachel, and therefore his actions do matter.

Rachel represents some kind of turning point in Will's life, as he now begins to think about what he does, to care about other people's feelings, and to show consideration to others. One could say that he has finally 'grown up'.

So both Rachel and Marcus teach Will how to treat others, but it is Rachel who is more important for Will since she touches his heart, while Marcus can be considered the catalyst that helped him to change or the bridge that connects him to others (p. 236, ll. 32–42).

4. Marcus and Fiona: The Mother–Son Relationship

The relationship between Marcus and Fiona is very complex. Students should become aware of the closeness between the two but also of the problems inherent in the relationship.

1. *Describe the mother–son relationship up to Chapter Nine.*

The detailed analysis of Ch. 1 should have made the students aware of the close relationship between Marcus and his mother. They are more like friends and talk to each other as if they were on equal terms.

Marcus's feelings towards his mother:
- Marcus is shown to be very caring and sensitive. He clearly feels responsible for his mother and is concerned about her well-being.
- However, he is too young to understand her psychological problems, and presumes that there is a logical reason for her misery – if only he could find it (p. 28, ll. 20–40).
- He does not feel able to discuss the problems he has at school with her, as she is mentally not equipped to deal with 'big stuff'. Yet as she is his mother, he feels she should be the person to help him (p. 41, ll. 58–66).
- Marcus almost seems to treat his mother like a child (p. 8, ll. 11–12; p. 41, ll. 67–68; p. 42, ll. 1–17).
- He blames her for many of his difficulties: 'he knew ... that he was weird because his mother was weird' (p. 16, ll. 15–16). She insists on him not behaving like other teenagers, so he is different, and this he blames squarely on her (p. 17, l. 47).

Fiona's attitude to Marcus:
- Fiona has no idea of Marcus's difficulties at school, much less of his sense of isolation. She gives him no support and just deals with his problems in an offhand way (about school: 'you'll get used to it', p. 15, l. 47).
- She seems to blame him for her problems ('we're not doing each other any good', p. 43, ll. 66–67)

Conclusion: The reader is given the feeling that the relationship is not working. Marcus cares deeply about his mother, but is exasperated by her. Yet she is the only person in his life, so he has to come to terms with her. Fiona is unaware of Marcus's misery as she is too wrapped up in her own problems.

2. *How does Fiona's suicide attempt change Marcus's attitude towards his mother?*

Fiona suffers from depression and is totally preoccupied with her own emotional problems, therefore her suicide attempt does not come as a big surprise.

It is, however, clearly a turning point in the mother–son relationship. Marcus is shattered when he realizes that his mother was about to leave him permanently. Moreover, his trust in Fiona (which had been a little shaky) has been destroyed (p. 65, ll. 56–58). Previously he never questioned her but now his attitude towards her begins to change. He begins to distance himself from her and realizes that he needs to find someone else so that he won't be on his own if anything does happen (p. 65, ll. 59–64).

3. *Re-read Fiona's farewell letter to her son (pp. 63–64). Imagine you are Marcus: Write a diary entry in which you explain your feelings about the incident.*

This activity can be done as a creative activity once the students have read Ch. 11, as many of Marcus's feelings about his mother and the suicide attempt are expressed in this chapter.

The suicide attempt has deeply traumatized Marcus and he cannot express his true feelings about it to anyone. Students should be aware of this when they draft their letter. The letter should be in line with Marcus's thoughts and language. While it should express his worries and fears, it should also reflect on the mother–son relationship from Marcus's point of view and perhaps mention his difficult situation at school.

4. *Describe Fiona's educational principles as depicted in Chapter 17 (pp. 111–116). How does the mother–son relationship change here?*

Role of a mother: Fiona is Marcus's mother and therefore, quite rightly, feels that she is the one who must decide who Marcus sees (p. 112, l. 1). She believes Marcus must talk to her rather than others about clothes, etc. (p. 112, ll. 5–6).

Non-conformist: The problem is that Fiona leads an alternative lifestyle, refusing to follow trends or fashion, and so has no idea what problems a teenager might face. She talks through issues with Marcus (p. 115, ll. 39–70) in an attempt to get him to 'think for himself'. She seems to treat him as an equal.

Authoritarian: However, as Marcus realizes, Fiona always wins their arguments and so Marcus always ends up doing what she wants him to do. Fiona automatically assumes that Marcus shares her tastes in such matters as music, clothing, food, computer games and vegetarianism (this has already been seen on p. 16, ll. 15–31). Significantly, Fiona is not aware that she is enforcing her beliefs on Marcus. In this section it is clear that their exchanges are very one-sided. At no point in their conversation does Fiona show genuine interest in Marcus's point of view. In fact, she completely fails to understand that her son's views differ from her own.

Consequences: As she is totally convinced of her own opinions, she fails to see Marcus's real needs. Instead, she mocks his desire to be like his fellow pupils and is unable, perhaps even unwilling, to see things from his point of view. This is one of the reasons why he is mercilessly bullied by others at school, and Marcus has already laid the blame for this partly on her (cf. p. 16, ll. 15–39).

Her inability to understand the true nature of Marcus's problems with his peers makes him seek out Will's friendship. It is by being with Will that Marcus learns how bad his situation at school really is. Gradually Marcus becomes more independent of his mother and dependent on Will. Ch. 17 marks a turning point as Marcus starts to express his doubts about his mother's views. He wins his first argument, employing the same strategy that she always uses: he strikes her a deadly verbal blow when he counters her criticism of his seeing Will by saying: 'I need a father' (p. 116, l. 5).

5. *Comment on Fiona's educational principles. Do you think she is a good mother?*

On the one hand, it could be argued that Fiona really does try to be a good mother. She wants Marcus to be a self-confident person who has a mind of his own and is free of materialistic consumer-oriented considerations. She really does want him to think for himself.

On the other hand, she does not let him develop his own tastes or preferences. Marcus is ridiculed at school and bullied because of the clothes he wears and because of his ignorance about contemporary teenage culture. As Fiona fails to realize the problems her views cause her son, she cannot be properly called 'a good mother'.

Should teachers wish to pursue this line of thought, they might have students discuss the best way of raising children so that they are not bullied, yet remain individualistic and able to look at things from a critical distance. The students working on this topic could then offer different solutions to the problem of how to be a good parent.

5. Marcus's Situation at School and His Friendship with Ellie

This topic concentrates on the issue of peer pressure and friendship. Firstly, Marcus's relationship with other pupils is examined (this should be done up to Ch. 16) and then his relationship with another, but rather different, teenager is examined (Ch. 19 onwards).

1. *What do we learn about Marcus's situation at school?*

From the beginning it is clear that Marcus does not fit in to school life. He suffers greatly at his new school in London and fears going there (pp. 14–15).

Problems:

- He looks different (his haircut, glasses and clothes are not trendy, p. 16, ll. 11–13).
- He behaves differently (he sometimes sings to himself in class, p. 17, ll. 47–61).
- He does not share the same interests as the others (he reads books, p. 17, ll. 40–46).

Consequences:

- He has got no friends and loses the few who do hang around with him (p. 29, ll. 49–69; p. 31, ll. 57ff.)
- He becomes the object of ridicule and bullying (p. 18, ll. 4–27; p. 30, ll. 13–55; p. 39, ll. 49ff.; p. 101, ll. 51ff.; p. 107, ll. 48–50).
- Marcus, who is shy and self-conscious, is not psychologically equipped to deal with the insults and aggression he encounters. He is helpless and withdraws into his own world, and tries to ignore his troubles (e.g. p. 30, ll. 15ff). However, even this does not work. It is Will who makes Marcus aware of some of the reasons why he is picked on (p. 94, ll. 23–68; pp. 104, ll. 17–33).

The various forms of bullying Marcus has to cope with should be collected and put on the board by the team dealing with this topic or should be the result of the classroom discussion following the student report:

- Marcus is laughed at and ridiculed by his schoolmates.
- His strangeness is used by the English teacher to make her class concentrate.
- He is rejected by Mark and Nicky.
- He is made to appear to be a shoplifter.
- He is followed after school and bombarded with sweets.
- He has his new Adidas trainers stolen.
- (Some boys steal his glasses.)

2. *Imagine you are a member of the student body that deals with bullying. Your task is to mediate conflicts. Work in teams of three to four and devise a strategy by which Marcus's situation could be changed for the better. The results can be presented either as a role-play or used in an open class discussion.*

3. *Why does the meeting with the headmistress (pp. 131–132) turn out to be a decisive moment in Marcus' life?*

The confrontation with the headmistress is a climax in a long series of humiliations Marcus has had to endure. Instead of helping the boy and trying to uncover the root of the problem, the headmistress only hands out meaningless advice ('couldn't you just try keeping out of their way?', p. 131, ll. 49–50).

Her lack of concern makes Marcus rebellious. He simply walks out on her, suddenly realizing that the forms of ostracism he finds himself confronted with are 'everything but normal' (p. 132, ll. 5–6). Thus Marcus begins to reject the notion that bullying is a natural state of affairs.

4. *How does his friendship with Ellie start to change Marcus's life?*

The beginnings of the friendship: Marcus meets Ellie McCrae by chance while waiting outside the headmistress's office. Ellie is a rebellious, rude, sulky and scruffy girl of 15 who is notorious for always being in trouble. Initially, Ellie does not take him seriously and makes fun of him. Marcus is not aware of the fact that she is mocking him and remains serious (pp. 128–130).

The relationship with Ellie does reveal some of Marcus's characteristics: not only is he lacking in self-confidence but he also has a good nature. He quite happily goes up to the feared Ellie to inform her that something she believed was not actually true – of course, he had failed to realize that Ellie was mocking him (pp. 139–140). Later he talks to her to ask if her boyfriend might beat him up (pp. 141–142).

However, it is when Ellie comes into his classroom to talk to him that Marcus's status among the other pupils changes. They fear Ellie, so are shocked when Ellie comes to find Marcus, who is either avoided or ridiculed by the rest of his class (pp. 143–145).

Later Ellie even defends him against two pupils who have taken his glasses and refuse to return them to Marcus (pp. 185–189).

Importance of the relationship: Ellie becomes important to Marcus for two reasons.

- Apart from Will she is the only other person Marcus can really talk to; she always fusses over him and seems pleased to see him.
- Marcus admires her brash ways and her self-assured manner. In this respect she functions as a model for him, as can be seen from the way he adopts some of her vulgar speech mannerisms like swearing (cf. topic 7 on p. 28 of the TM). It is by being with her that Marcus becomes more outspoken, self-confident and, finally, more of a normal teenager.

Why Ellie likes Marcus:

- Ellie accepts Marcus as he is. She finds his strangeness amusing but is not nasty about it. 'Boys are peculiar creatures. Not you, though, Marcus. Well, you're peculiar, but in a different way.' (p. 187, ll. 42–44).
- She is different from other teenagers because she projects a strong image of herself. But she no more pretends than Marcus does. Both are honest, whereas most teenagers – as Will remarks (p. 104, ll. 23–24) – hide behind an image. Ellie does not put on an act; she is who she is (p. 142, ll. 28–35).
- She talks to him easily (pp. 165–171). As she is not worried about her image, she does not feel insecure because of Marcus's weirdness. Pupils often bully others because they recognize in them the insecurities that they are trying to hide. Marcus's strangeness is too obvious for everyone.
- He appeals to her protective nature (p. 186, ll. 32–46). Despite her strong character, she also has a naturally affectionate side and hugs him eagerly (p. 165, ll. 32–33; p. 170, l. 7; p. 198, ll. 33–35).
- She takes him seriously, talking about 'big' things in an easy unforced manner (p. 168, ll. 1–52) and is prepared to accept the fact that Marcus knows things she does not understand (p. 200, ll. 6–42). When he says he wants to talk to her, she is prepared to listen (pp. 212, ll. 23ff.).

Conclusion: Ellie's influence on Marcus:

- She makes him aware of the importance of music like grunge to teenagers.
- She stops other boys from bullying him, thereby becoming his protector.
- She becomes his friend, his confidante.
- She teaches him to behave like a teenager.
- For a while she is a role-model for him.

5. *Why does Marcus finally come to the conclusion that Ellie would not be an appropriate girlfriend for him?*

Differences:

- Marcus realizes that he needs to be with 'someone quieter, someone who liked reading and computer games' (p. 226, ll. 9–10), someone who does not consider life to be 'shit' (p. 227, l. 45), someone who is 'less different' (p. 242, l. 30).
- The fact that Marcus and Ellie are opposites means that they have an attraction for each other (p. 226, ll. 13–20), but in the long run it 'wasn't an awful lot of fun' (p. 226, l. 21).

Ellie's character:

- When Marcus and Ellie go by train to Cambridge, Marcus realizes for the first time that Ellie is unpredictable, erratic and, as he puts it, 'scary' (p. 218, l. 13). When he earlier described her as 'scary' (p. 168, l. 18), he meant she scared people.
- She makes life difficult for herself: 'Ellie spent her whole time wanting life to be shit, and then making life shit by making things difficult for herself' (p. 227, ll. 48–49).

Conclusion: Despite her strengths, Ellie has little, if any, self-esteem, whilst Marcus is just discovering his own worth. The realization that he needs someone who is less different from him signals Marcus's new self-awareness and the fact that he is growing up emotionally.

6. The Stages of Marcus's Development

1. *Summarize in your own words Marcus's situation up to his mother's suicide attempt.*

- Twelve-year-old Marcus has no friends whatsoever.
- He is an outsider at his new school, the other pupils make fun of him and sometimes even bully him.
- His divorced mother is becoming increasingly unhappy, she is depressed and is unable to help Marcus, as she is so wrapped up in her problems.

2. *How does Fiona's suicide attempt change Marcus's life?*

- Returning home from the SPAT outing, Suzie, Will and Marcus find the unconscious Fiona lying on the floor. Outwardly, Marcus reacts in a very controlled manner (p. 56, ll. 14–15). Inwardly, he is frightened and knows that this is 'the scariest thing he's ever seen' (p. 57, ll. 42–43).
- He is afraid that his mother might attempt suicide again (p. 58, ll. 24–32; p. 65, ll. 44–47) and this fear haunts his life ('What he felt, all the time, every single day, was a horrible fear', p. 96, ll. 26–27). Moreover, he suspects that he might be the reason for the attempted suicide (p. 56, ll. 29–30; p. 59, ll. 44–47).
- For the first time Marcus wishes to be part of a family and he decides to find a boyfriend for his mother so that she will feel better and won't be sad any more (p. 65, ll. 59–64; p. 76, ll. 1–17; p. 81, ll. 49–66).
- However, Marcus's attempts to get his mother and Will together fail (pp. 81–87).
- Once he realizes that Will has not got a son, Marcus even tries to blackmail him into going out with his mother (p. 89, ll. 52–53).

Conclusion: Thus the first stage of Marcus's development may be described as a change from passivity and lethargy to initiative and resourcefulness.

3. *Show how Marcus's life is transformed by his friendship with Will.*

- Significantly, Will becomes Marcus's first confidant. They not only talk about school (p. 93, ll. 66ff.) but, more importantly, about Marcus's bad experiences at school (p. 94, ll. 9–68; p. 102–104).
- Will explains to Marcus that part of the latter's problem is that he sticks out due to his terrible clothes and haircut (p. 94, ll. 37–53).
- Will is the only person to inquire about Marcus's mum (p. 96, ll. 8–45); he also asks him about his dad (p. 99, ll. 47ff.).
- Once he realizes that Will is not going to go out with his mother, Marcus still continues to visit Will. Will becomes a refuge from the fears he has that his mother may kill herself (p. 96, ll. 27–44); Will is the right person to deal with Marcus's fears precisely because he is so emotionally distant; he is more like a friend of the same age than an adult.
- Will understands what teenagers need (p. 112, l. 11) and buys Marcus his first trendy clothes – a pair of trainers (p. 104, ll. 34ff.).
- Being with someone who has such a different experience of life from that of his parents allows Marcus to begin to examine his own way of life and to question some of his mother's principles. He wants to know why he is a vegetarian and to decide things for himself and for the first time manages to get his mother to shut up and accept his point of view (pp. 113–116). What may at first glance appear to be part of a normal teenager's rebellion, has, however, a deeper significance: Marcus has started to lose some of his fear and has begun to deal with his mother's limitations successfully.

4. *Explain how the friendship with Ellie contributes to Marcus's emotional and mental growth.*

- Like Will, Ellie acts as a kind of mentor for Marcus. She is the first adolescent Marcus has long conversations with, she becomes fond of him in a protective way and defends him against pupils who bully him (cf. topic 5, p. 24 of the TM).
- When his mother has a new bout of depression, Marcus for the first time realizes he is no longer alone: 'He had Will, he had Ellie, ... he had two friends' (p. 195, ll. 26–27).
- Being with Ellie provides Marcus with new insights. Having a close friendship with a rebellious character is a new experience, but it also makes him grow up mentally and emotionally. After Ellie's immature reaction to the poster of Kurt Cobain in the record shop and his stay at the police station, Marcus becomes aware of how much he has changed and also how he needs someone who is a little bit more like himself (p. 226, ll. 5–24).
- In his conversation with his father he expresses his newly acquired sense of belonging through the image of the human pyramid (p. 247, ll. 50–53), an idea that he repeats to Will (p. 251, ll. 59–69). What Marcus has learned is to cope with his own life and to have a more optimistic outlook on life and on his own future.

The individual stages of his development are illustrated in the graph on the next page. This can be worked through in class with the students.

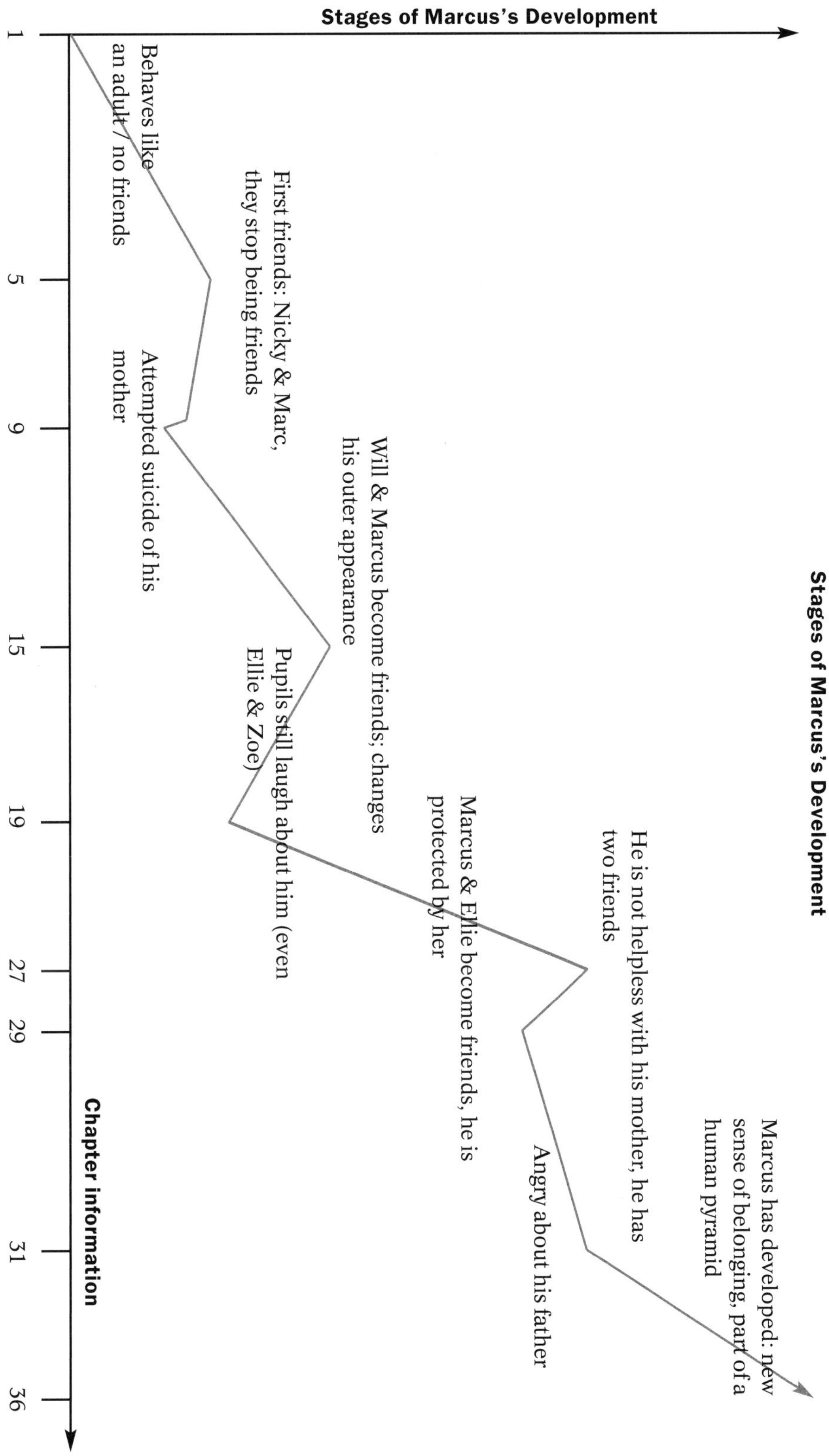
Stages of Marcus's Development
Chapter information
1
5
9
15
19
27
29
31
36
Behaves like an adult / no friends
First friends: Nicky & Marc, they stop being friends
Attempted suicide of his mother
Will & Marcus become friends; changes his outer appearance
Pupils still laugh about him (even Ellie & Zoe)
Marcus & Ellie become friends, he is protected by her
He is not helpless with his mother, he has two friends
Angry about his father
Marcus has developed: new sense of belonging, part of a human pyramid

7. Marcus: An Analysis of His Language

From the analysis of the first four chapters students should have realized that Marcus is precocious, is somewhat different from his peers and could well be described as 'weird'. The work on the other topics will have shown that he has undergone distinct changes and that Will and Ellie are the driving forces behind his development.

Naturally the changes in Marcus are also reflected in his way of talking. Of all the topics, the analysis of Marcus's language is perhaps the most demanding; it will most certainly be the least popular among students. Hence additional help by the teacher is likely to be necessary; alternatively, the teacher may prefer a teacher-based approach from the beginning, or may indeed embed this topic in some of the other topics.

1. *Analyse Marcus's language and communication strategies. What do you notice?*

Below are a list of features that students should become aware of while reading the novel, as they form an important part in Marcus's characterization.

Questions:

- The novel opens with a question ('Have you split up now?'). It is about his mother and her boyfriend breaking up. Marcus proceeds to question Fiona about her relationship and the reasons why she and her boyfriend have broken up. It is a delicate matter, and while others might not broach the subject, Marcus inquires directly about it. One would not expect a 12-year-old to ask his mother so directly and matter-of-factly about her love life. This character trait is probably encouraged by his mother ('they'd had lots to talk about London, and the changes that were happening to them, and how they were all for the best probably', p. 7, ll. 67–69)
- Later on in the chapter, however, he asks questions about how to deal with the three pizzas in roughly the same manner as he has dealt with his mother's relationship. He does not change the emotional level for questions of food or for questions of love, revealing his inability to understand the need of people to deal with varying matters on different levels.
- Marcus often forces his dialogue partner to be precise, e.g. when he asks his mother, 'What kind of sick?' (p. 41, l. 40) or when Will says casually that it is a shame that he does not like football, he bluntly asks 'Why?' (p. 49, l. 48), to which there is no real answer.
- When Will is trying to be polite, Marcus asks 'Are you getting these questions out of a book?' (p. 49, l. 51), which causes Will to blush. Marcus does not seem to take other people's feelings into account.
- He is confrontational with Suzie who is trying to make him feel better at the hospital: 'How do you know?' (p. 59, l. 47).
- After his mother returns from hospital, Marcus assaults her with questions. Obviously, he is entitled to do so, but a more sensitive person might have worried more about the weak state of mind of a person who has just attempted suicide (p. 64, ll. 19; p. 65, ll. 45–46).
- Marcus forces Will to discuss his feelings for Fiona and Suzie (p. 89, ll. 59–61).
- When Will is trying to find out about the bullying at school, Marcus only answers each individual question or responds to the particular statement Will makes (pp. 102, ll. 22ff.). He is unable to understand what Will is driving at. Finally he says 'You could have just asked' (p. 103, l. 58). Marcus cannot go beyond his own particular and peculiar strategy for gathering information, so cannot respond as any normal person might to Will's delicate questioning. As Will says, Marcus is 'literal-minded' (p. 103, l. 51).
- Marcus also uses question tags often, but he does not employ the tags to invite his listener to join in the conversation. Instead, his tags are used in a preemptory manner, they literally freeze out his dialogue partner (p. 60, ll. 33–34).

Questions are a natural part of dialogue but Marcus's questions serve to unsettle others. They are direct and also reveal a lack of tact in understanding other people.

Words and feelings:

- However, Marcus's directness is also an indication that he cannot use language creatively, which is why euphemisms and irony do not form a part of his language. This is apparent when he corrects Suzie's euphemistic description of Fiona as being 'under the weather' and 'off colour' by simply saying 'I call it nuts' (p. 50, l. 18).
- In his conversation on the phone with Will, it becomes apparent that Marcus cannot deal with sarcasm ('Sarcasm … was a language that Marcus found peculiarly baffling', p. 74, ll. 17–19).
- Marcus cannot understand that irony is a way of informing someone that what they think is stupid. When Will says to Fiona, 'Give him a couple of weeks and he'll be OK, eh? Once they've stopped stealing his shoes and following him home from school everything will be great.' (p. 110, ll. 32–34), and then explains to Marcus that he was joking, Marcus finds it inappropriate to joke during this conversation (p. 110, ll. 38–39).
- Ch. 13 contains a good example of Marcus failing to understand how conversations work. Firstly, Will has to go through a long discussion about where to

eat (p. 79, ll. 42ff.) in order to change Marcus's mind about where to eat. Then Marcus tries to get the adults to talk, although he reveals he has no idea how conversations are supposed to take place 'Don't just sit there ... Talk to each other' (p. 81, ll. 67–69).
- Marcus's entire conversations in Ch. 21 with Ellie revolve around her teasing him without him realizing she is making fun of him.
- One interesting reflection by Marcus is on the difference between Ali's threats and his inner fears. Marcus is unable to grasp that a person may say something that bears no relationship to their feelings (p. 184, ll. 16–26). Marcus says what he feels, and does not hide his insecurities.

Register:
- Occasionally his language is very formal, even stilted. Note the following: 'If you can't look after me properly then you'll have to find someone who can.' These words would clearly be more appropriate for an officer from the youth welfare office than for a 12-year-old boy. Another example is: 'Well, I wouldn't describe myself as an expert' (p. 175, l. 56) when discussing love.
- When his mother is depressed, they reverse roles and he talks to her as if he is the parent and she the child (p. 40, ll. 38–40; p. 41, ll. 67–70; p. 42, ll. 1–17)
- Nevertheless, his vocabulary is often revealed to be that of a normal 12-year-old. He does not understand long or difficult words like 'cynic' (p. 83, l. 45), 'melodramatic' (p. 111, l. 44) or 'patronize' (p. 252, l. 14).

Problem area:
- Marcus has only one area where he fears communication: his mother's suicide. While he can talk about it with her directly afterwards (p. 64, ll. 15ff.), he later never mentions the subject, being unable to talk to others about it (p. 96, ll. 10–44, with his 'I dunno', l. 37, being one of the few straight lies he tells) nor indeed to mention it to his own mother (p. 66, ll. 20ff.) – calling it 'the ... thing' (p. 68, l. 6). Nor does he want others to talk about it in case it has a bad effect on his mother (p. 111, ll. 51–59). Again later, he does not want his dad to find out about his mum (p. 232, ll. 1–14).

Conclusion: Whereas most people develop intricate and subtle linguistic strategies for dealing with complex emotional issues, Marcus is blunt to the point of causing embarassment. He is direct in trying to find information, whereas others tend to be more discrete.

Instead of making him stronger, however, this makes him more vulnerable, as he is incapable of dealing with things in a roundabout way.

2. *Analyse Ellie's manner of speaking and compare it with Marcus's. What differences can you detect? What does it reveal about Marcus?*

Ellie uses four-letter words and swears e.g. 'squitty shitty snotty bastard' (p. 128, l. 36), 'fucking' (p. 129, ll. 41, 53) and is generally rude and aggressive (p. 128–130; p. 141, ll. 59–61).

She is rude about and to her mother, even though she likes her (p. 166, ll. 9–15; p. 170, ll. 27–41)

By contrast, Marcus's language is, for the most part, totally devoid of slang and vulgar expressions. It is as if he has no teenage jargon at his disposal. The conversation between Ellie and Marcus in front of the headmistress's office highlights the difference in language and attitude between the two.

It is noticeable that in his thoughts he occasionally, however, does use vulgar language, but in a way that reveals that he has analysed and understood the way others use vulgar language (p. 43, ll. 40–44).

Marcus is mostly blunt but not deliberately rude to those around him.

3. *How does Marcus's language change? What do these changes signify?*

As the action progresses and as Marcus increasingly detaches himself from Fiona, changes in his language may be observed. He does develop a sense of humour, which only once really breaks out into the open (p. 178, ll. 29–35), when he realizes how ridiculous he is (laughing about oneself is an important part of being able to look at oneself with detachment) and occasionally even employs rude words 'piss off' (p. 211, l. 52) and 'shit' (p. 229, l. 50); these one can presume, he has picked up from hanging around with Ellie (p. 211, ll. 54–55). Hence his manner of speaking reflects his emotional change.

His first rebellion is against Mrs Morrison, but it is because he is unable to express his frustration about her lack of empathy, so he just says, 'I've finished with you' (p. 131, l. 62).

He is prepared to be rude to his parents: 'you are a useless father' (p. 232, l. 35), 'Shut up, Mum. You're mad. Bloody hell, I can't believe how crap my parents are', p. 241, ll. 62–63) – and to Lindsey 'And you can shut up' (p. 233, l. 41). This must be seen as Marcus's coming of age; not that swearing and being rude is the significant part, but that he is prepared to stop hiding in the shadows and feels able to express his frustration and anger, and to let others know what he thinks of them. He refuses to let adults patronize him any more.

However, it should be noted that Marcus has not completely replaced his formal register with teenage jargon. He retains some of his 'old' ways of speaking ('I just don't think couples are the future', p. 252, l. 5), but his wording has become less stilted and artificial.

Marcus's language at the beginning	*Ellie's language*	*Marcus's language at a later stage*
direct, matter-of-fact: 'So have you split up now?' (p. 5) 'It looks to me like you've split up. But I just wanted to make sure.' (p. 5) **question tags:** 'You want to go out with Suzie, don't you?' (p. 89)	**direct, intending to be impolite** 'I haven't got a bloody clue who you are.' (p. 129) 'You're disgusting. Forty-three years old and you're snogging against a garden shed.' (p. 170)	**direct, less polite but honest** 'I suppose you are a useless father, and that doesn't help a kid very much, but you'd have been a useless father wherever you were living' (p. 232)
very formal, stilted: 'If you can't look after me properly then you'll have to find someone who can.' (p. 42) 'I wouldn't really describe myself as an expert' (p. 175) **understatement:** 'Good. Thank you. I have to admit I was a bit worried when he said that.' (p. 142)	**slang:** 'I haven't got a bloody clue who you are.' (p. 129) 'How come every squitty little shitty snotty bastard knows my name?' (p. 128) **four-letter words:** 'Don't be so fucking rude.' (p. 129)	**slang (like any normal teenager):** 'He can piss off' (p. 211) 'I bloody hate Joni Mitchell.' (p. 255) **But also his 'old' language:** 'Because ... You know when they do those human pyramids? That's the sort of model for living I'm looking at now.' (p. 251) 'I just don't think couples are the future.' (p. 252)
wants his conversation partner to be more precise: 'Didn't you go to work today?' (p. 40) 'What kind of sick?' (p. 41)		
no jokes (and no understanding of irony/sarcasm)	**irony/jokes:** M: 'Kurt Cobain doesn't play ...' E.: 'Oh no! Have they got rid of him?' (p. 139)	
→ no teenage jargon, formal register reflecting his precociousness	→ informal register, teenage jargon	→ use of different registers reflecting his change

Creative Approaches to the Novel

Creative approaches are especially important if the class is reading the novel in a chronological manner. For students working in study groups, it may be helpful if the teacher suggests creative ways that the students might present information to the class, as a pure analysis of a topic might not arouse the interest of everyone in the class. Besides the ideas suggested under the section 'Topics' (cf. pp. 14–30), some of the following ideas may be incorporated.

Freeze Frames

Besides allowing the students a full physical reaction to a novel (the importance of which should not be underestimated for restless teenagers), freeze frames also make the students think about action and character.

The following episodes might make for good freeze frames (the exact moment of the freeze frame should be decided on by the students). The teacher can suggest them to a group of students who then enact them in front of the class. The other students (who obviously must know which chapter is being dealt with) can discuss the feelings and motivations of the characters.

Chapter Nine (p. 55, ll. 63 – p. 57, ll. 57)
Chapter Thirteen (p. 81, l. 67 – p. 82, l. 25)
Chapter Sixteen (p. 101, l. 51 – p. 101, l. 64)
Chapter Nineteen (p. 128, l. 11 – p. 130, l. 35)
Chapter Twenty-four (p. 161, l. 60 – p. 162, l. 26)
Chapter Twenty-six (p. 180)
Chapter Thirty-three (p. 229, ll. 39–70)

Creative Writing

Besides the tasks suggested under the 'Topics', the following could be useful for developing writing skills.

Chapter 12
Choose one of the jobs Will wrote a letter of application for. Then write his letter of application and his CV.
[This activity is not easy, as the students will have to use persuasive language in his letter of application and invent (and as it is Will, probably lie about) his life and work.]

Chapter 19
- Imagine you are Mrs Morrison. Write either:
  a) A report to Ellie's mother about Ellie's behaviour at school;
  or
  b) A report to Fiona Brewer about Marcus.

Chapter 24
- Imagine you are Rachel. Write an email to a girlfriend a few days after the New Year's Eve Party where you met Will. Talk about the party and your impressions of Will.

Chapter 33
The class should be divided into groups, with one half writing the first and the other half the second writing activities:
- Write a report of no more than 200 words for the *Royston Gazette* about the incident in Royston High Street.
- You are a middle-aged conservative person who has read the report in the *Royston Gazette*. Write a letter-to-the-editor about the report.

Turning an Episode into a Series of Storyboards for a Film

As the novel has been turned into a film and the class at some stage will probably wish to see the film (cf. p. 35), it would be a good idea to prepare the class beforehand by giving them an activity that examines the transformation of a written text into a film. This will make them aware of the differences between the two media and allow them to approach the film more critically than would be the case if they were merely passive spectators. Quite what the results of this activity may be depends on the class. The material printed below and on p. 33 is taken from a student report and may serve as an example, since it indicates what can reasonably be expected.

Students should be familiar with the language of film analysis and the genre if this activity is to be successful. This should be the case in those *bundesländer*, in which the genre of film has already been introduced. Should teachers feel the need to help their students in this area, there are glossaries in the following Cornelsen publications:

- *English Eleven 2000*, pp. 78–80 (Best.-Nr. 358160)
- *Level Crossing*, pp. 73–75 (Best.-Nr. 63658)
- *Across Cultures*, pp. 67–69 (Best.-Nr. 371760).

Before embarking on this topic, it would be useful for the class to examine a short sequence from a film (examples can be found in the above-mentioned books) to work out how best they can do this activity (besides being useful as an introduction to film vocabulary). For this reason, it should be emphasized that, despite what many students might think, this is in no way an easy task. The students should work in small groups for it to be successful. How they present their material to the class should also be discussed with the teacher in detail. Some students may want to take the storyboards further and convert them into a short film sequence; certainly the teacher should discuss with them what might and can be expected (and perhaps advise them to avoid trying to make a really professional film out of their material). The students could be given the following tasks to help them sort out their thoughts:

- *Explain your choice of scene.*
- *Explain your choice of actors, your shots and camera angles and the effect you wish to create.*

Example:
End of Chapter Eight and the whole of Chapter Nine
Reasons for choice: We chose Chapter Nine for our film script because we think that it is one of the most important chapters in the novel.

On the one hand, it is the first time that Will and Marcus meet. On the other hand, Marcus's mother Fiona tries to commit suicide and Marcus realizes that this is something he will have to deal with for the rest of his life. Moreover, because of this incident Marcus wishes to have a larger family for the first time.

So Marcus's and Will's life and their future are influenced by the action in this chapter. It is now that their lives start to change.

Film script
Starting point: The people of SPAT (Single Parents – Alone Together) are having a picnic in Regent's Park on a Saturday. Will, Suzie, Megan and Marcus join the group. While Marcus is walking around the boating lake, he throws pieces of bread at the ducks. Suzie and Will in the meantime talk to each other. Suddenly Marcus comes up to them.

(Cf. storyboard on opposite page)

Ideally, all of Chapter Nine is transformed in this way. The team illustrate some of their shots, present the effect they wish to create and explain their choice of actors.

They might discuss other areas of film-making, like what background music could accompany the scenes (if any), what clothes the actors should be wearing, what hairstyles, etc.

Shots	***Action/dialogues***	***Camera work***
1	Marcus runs to the group (to Suzie, Megan and Will).	**Setting:** Regent's Park. **Characters:** Will, Suzie, Megan, Marcus. **Camera angle:** High-angle shot. **Camera range:** Long shot. Marcus is filmed from a high-angle shot. You can see the whole surroundings of the park, as Marcus runs from the edge of the lake. Slowly the camera pans down so you can see Will and Suzie talking. This way you get an overview, a first impression of the situation.
2	Suddenly Marcus is in front of Will and Suzie. He skips from foot to foot and seems to be very nervous. He says: 'I think I've killed a duck.'	**Camera angle:** Low-angle shot from Will's point of view (Will and Suzie are sitting on the grass). **Camera range:** *First:* Full shot of Marcus, to show him hopping from foot to foot, to emphasize his nervousness. *Then:* Close-up of Marcus's face, to show his anxious expression. He cannot believe what he has done and he is really stunned and shocked.
3	Will and Suzie look at Marcus. Megan is sleeping in her pram.	**Camera angle:** Reverse-angle shot. It shows the scene from Marcus's point of view. This way you can see the reactions of Will and Suzie at what Marcus is saying. **Camera range:** Medium-long shot. It shows Will, Suzie and Megan together in the park and other members of SPAT behind them, sitting on blankets under a tree. Will and Suzie seem to be very surprised and look blankly at Marcus.
4	Will, Suzie and Marcus go to the lake to see what Marcus has done. Suzie pushes Megan, who is sleeping in her pram.	**Camera movement:** Tracking shot. The camera is in front of the four people. **Camera range:** *First:* Medium shot of the group. Will and Suzie are silent. They are thinking about what has happened. *Then:* Close-up of Marcus's face. It emphasizes that Marcus is very thoughtful (he is lost in thought).
5	They are standing on the path at the edge of the lake, staring at the dead duck floating in the water.	**Camera angle:** Point-of-view shot. It shows the scene from Will's point of view. **Camera range:** *First:* Long shot. It shows something floating in the water, but the camera is at a great distance from the subject. *Then:* The camera zooms in and you see in a medium shot that there really is a dead duck floating in the water.

Writing a Review

Writing a review is always a rewarding writing task. Depending on the ability of the students, the teacher can either ask them to write a personal review or a more formal book review. Depending on which the teacher wants the class to write, the students should first of all be asked to develop their own ideas as to what a review should be like. These ideas can be collected on the board and put into a structured sequence.

If the students want to write a personal review, they should be asked to consider whether they want to recommend the book or advise others not to read it, and they should choose aspects they wish to praise or criticize.

Before writing their review, it might be useful for them to read some other personal reviews. There is a link at the www.learnetix.de/bookshelf website under the heading 'About a Boy', where it says 'Here you can read other readers' reviews of *About a Boy*'. Here they will find reviews which are intended for quick public consumption.

If the teacher wants the class to write a more formal review, then Infosheet 2 (p. 44) should be given to the students to help them (once their own ideas have been discussed). Again, it would be useful for the students to read some reviews beforehand, so that they have an idea of how they are structured and what elements reviewers mention. At the Learnetix 'About a Boy' site there are several reviews. The students should be told to scan them in order to work out what information they contain, rather than read them for detail.

Students are then asked to write their own reviews at home. These can serve as a final assessment of the novel: they may be hung up on the wall, discussed in small groups or exchanged among students and become the basis for a letter-to-the-editor.

Working with the Film in the Classroom

In 2002 Universal released the film version of *About a Boy*. It was directed by Chris and Paul Weitz and starred Hugh Grant, Toni Collette, Rachel Weisz and Nicholas Hoult.

The film deviates in many ways from the novel, but is still as enjoyable the novel. The fact that it deviates so much allows for an interesting classroom discussion about why changes were made and how successful these changes are.

This section contains information about how to work with the film and offers a synopsis of the film. The scenes are those the DVD is divided into, and it is strongly recommended that the teacher acquires the DVD, as it makes the work for the teacher (and the students) easier.

It is suggested that the film is shown and discussed after the novel has been thoroughly dealt with in the classroom. In this way classroom work can concentrate on how the novel has been transformed into another medium and one need not do extensive comprehension exercises, as the students can easily follow the dialogues.

Synopsis of the film *About a Boy*

Scene One (00:00–6:32)
Will is introduced wandering around his expensively and stylishly furnished flat, while watching a quiz show (*Who Wants To Be a Millionaire?*) on TV. The question asked is about the author of the phrase 'no man is an island' (John Donne), a phrase Will does not agree with. The film shows from the beginning how Will is self-centred and cut off from others.

There is a cut to Marcus, the second main character; we hear Marcus's voice and soon realize that he is talking while lying in bed at night: 'I didn't fit into my old school and I certainly don't fit into my new school'. With these lines the role of Marcus as an outsider is established.

Will drives off in his sports car to a couple who have a newborn baby. He is asked to be the child's godfather, which he turns down.

Marcus who is walked to his new school by his mother. His hippy, untrendy clothes clearly set him apart from his fellow students, who ridicule him.

Scene Two (6:33–10:32)
Will meets a date (Angie) in a restaurant; she tells him that she has a three-year-old son; Will pretends to love kids. Will's affair with Angie is then shown in quick cuts. When Angie ends the relationship (differently from the end of his other relationships) it dawns on Will that single mothers might turn out to be ideal sex partners.

Scene Three (10:33–12:50)
Fiona is crying and seems unable to prepare breakfast for Marcus. The next two episodes are set at Marcus's school: Marcus starts singing in class without realizing what he is doing and is ridiculed by the other pupils; in the playground he is bullied by some pupils and then rejected by his friends as they don't want to have any contact with him.

Scene Four (12:51–17:07)
We see Will shopping in a supermarket; he is wondering where to find beautiful single mothers when he comes across an advert for SPAT. He goes to a meeting of the self-help group; we see him sitting in a circle with women who have been abandoned by their partners, and he starts inventing stories about his son. A young woman, Suzie, agrees to go with him to the SPAT picnic. Will goes and buys a children's seat for his car which he then makes dirty.

Scene Five (17:08–20:11)
Will picks up Suzie and her baby for an outing in the park. Marcus is accompanying them as his mother is supposedly not well. They learn from Will that he lives off the royalties of his father's famous Christmas song. The close-ups of her face indicate her incredulity and perhaps an implicit criticism of Will who confesses to have never worked in his life. Up to this point the atmosphere is carefree and joyful.

Scene Six (20:12–22:24)
Marcus is standing in front of a pond with ducks swimming around. He throws the inedible bread his mother has baked into the water and kills a duck. When the park-keeper appears, Will defends Marcus, saying that the duck was dead. Suddenly Marcus thinks he sees his mother standing on the other side of the pond.

Scene Seven (22:25–28:35)
Will is taking Marcus home. Suzie, Marcus and Will enter the flat and find the unconscious Fiona lying on a sofa. It becomes apparent that she has taken an overdosis of pills.

Will follows the ambulance to the hospital, then we see them in the hospital's waiting room. They are informed by the nurse that Fiona is all right; Will takes Marcus, Suzie and her baby to Suzie's flat.

Scene Eight (28:35–33:45)
The scene begins with an overview of Will's way of life. We see him making an espresso, lying in the bath tub, watching TV, being online or playing billiard. Will explains his lifestyle ('the important thing in island living is to be your own activities director') and justifies his not wanting to have any children or work. When he is at the hairdresser's his mobile rings and Marcus persuades him to treat Fiona and himself to dinner in a restaurant.

Will, Fiona and Marcus go to a restaurant, where it is clear that Will and Marcus have a different view of Fiona. Later at their flat Will is driven crazy by Fiona and Marcus's music.

Scene Nine (33:46–42:15)
This is, in many respects, the turning point in the development of the plot. At the beginning, Will has this to say about himself: 'Me, I didn't mean anything. About anything, to anyone. And I knew that guaranteed me a long, depression-free life.' As he is to discover, he does mean something to someone. Marcus is shadowing Will in the streets, follows him to a supermarket, rings the doorbell of Will's flat and confronts him with his earlier lie about his invented son. He blackmails Will into letting him visit regularly; the frequent visits which Will has come to tolerate show us that he is slowly becoming involved in Marcus's life, that he is beginning to stop shying away from any form of commitment.

The various episodes inside Will's stylish flat are interrupted by a brief episode in which we see Fiona and Marcus outside on the street; both are wearing hand-woven, woollen caps which contrast markedly with the clothes of fashion-conscious Will and remind us of the incompatibility of Fiona's and Will's ways of life.

Marcus and Will talk about Fiona, and later about Will's dad.

Scene Ten (42:15–45:37)
Marcus is at school walking down a staircase, followed by pupils who throw things at him. An abrupt cut bring us to Will's flat; he is watching an animal film on TV. Suddenly the doorbell rings, Marcus is outside, some boys are throwing sweets at him. Will takes Marcus inside and asks him about this form of bullying. He learns that Marcus is having a hard time at school.

For the first time, Will seems to be really concerned. He takes Marcus to a store and buys him a pair of trendy shoes, realizing all of a sudden that 'this was what people meant by a natural high . ... I had made an unhappy boy temporarily happy.'

Scene Eleven (45:37–50:15)
A shoeless Marcus is standing in the rain in front of his house. Once inside, he has to explain to his mother that his shoes were stolen. Gradually Fiona discovers from her son that Marcus goes to see Will every afternoon after school and that he was bought a pair of trendy trainers. Enraged she storms out of the house, dragging Marcus with her. She goes to look for Will in the restaurant that he usually goes to. There is a row between between Fiona and Will, as she is implying that Will is a homosexual who is molesting young boys. During the quarrel Will tries to make Fiona aware of some of Marcus's problems at school. Throughout the dialogue the imagery of the island is used again. Fiona maintains that 'no man is an island', while Will angrily replies: 'I am an island. I'm a very cool island.' The episode ends with Marcus inviting Will to their Christmas party.

Scene Twelve (50:15–55:51)
Will is in a shopping mall. He says to himself that he has no intention whatsoever of accepting Marcus's invitation. Rather, he intends to spend Christmas as he always does: watching a video and getting drunk and high. Next we see Will in a video shop in front of the horror movie section, then in front of his own TV watching a Frankenstein version with Boris Karloff.

There is a cut to Fiona's flat; an uncomfortable Will is sitting together with Marcus's father, his new girlfriend and her mother. Their attire and way of speaking show that they are not trendy.

After the exchange of presents Suzie arrives, greeting Will rather frostily and starts to make fun of him. Embarrassed, Will wants to leave, but Marcus defends him, so he stays. Will admits to himself over Christmas dinner that he was enjoying himself.

Scene Thirteen (55:15–1:00:05)
At a New Year's Eve party Will falls in love with Rachel. Marcus meets Ellie at school.

Scene Fourteen (1:00:05–1:06:24)
Will goes to see Marcus and asks for his help while they are strolling around a zoo. He wants him to pretend to be his son when he meets Rachel. Will is embarrassed by having to ask somebody for something.

The scene then shifts to Rachel's home. Marcus has to go up to Ali's room, who clearly dislikes him and wants him out of the house.

Will is mesmerized by Rachel. Meanwhile, Marcus has left Rachel's house, but is brought back by Will. Ali apologizes to Marcus. The episode ends on an amusing note when Marcus tells Rachel that Will 'fancies' her.

Scene Fifteen (1:06:24–1:10:53)
The scene is made up of five different episodes. First we see Marcus and Ellie outside school, walking down a pavement; Ellie puts her arm around Marcus in a friendly gesture. Next Will and Marcus play billiards together; they talk about Rachel and Ellie; Marcus confronts Will with the fact that he has deceived Rachel, that he does not tell the truth, i.e. telling her that Marcus is not his son. The confrontation deeply affects Will; lying on his sofa in his flat he ponders about what Marcus has told him. Will decides to tell her the truth. The fourth part of this chapter is set in a restaurant; it is difficult for Will to be honest with Rachel, while Rachel is perplexed and hurt. Will slowly gets up, looking utterly defeated, and leaves the restaurant. There is a final fade-in to his flat, we see him sitting alone on his sofa, not doing anything.

Scene Sixteen (1:10:53–1:16:23)
Marcus is at school in the schoolyard; he walks home, opens the door and finds his mother sitting on the sofa and crying. Nothing is said, but Marcus is worried. After a maths lesson, Marcus tells Ellie he would like to play at the school's rock concert, but Ellie discourages him, saying he would make a fool of himself. Marcus visits Will and tells him about his mum, but Will says he cannot help. Marcus becomes angry and says that Will doesn't 'give a shit about anybody.' There is a cut, the scene shifts to Marcus'school again, we see him signing up for the rock concert. He is shown alone and isolated.

Scene Seventeen (1:16:23–1:22:20)
Will is also alone and desperate; his voice-over narration contributes to this impression. Suddenly it dawns on him that 'Marcus was the only thing that meant something to me' and as Fiona matters to Marcus, he decides to help her. He rushes to Fiona's house, only to find a note which informs him that she is at a SPAT meeting. He learns that Marcus is singing at a school concert, and together they rush off in Will's car. Will succeeds in making Fiona realize that Marcus's musical performance will be disastrous because he is only following his mother's musical taste and will be ridiculed by his fellow pupils. Will leaves his car with Fiona and runs into the school building.

Scene Eighteen (1:22:20–1:30:04)
We see enthusiastic parents and pupils at the 'kidz rock' concert. Will is making his way through the crowd, looking for Marcus. He briefly speaks to Rachel, whose son Ali is doing a performance. The curtain closes, and a teacher steps in front to announce Marcus's solo of 'Killing Me Softly'. There is laughter in the audience. Will tries to discourage Marcus from going on stage; Marcus insists ('It'll make her [my mum] happy'), and goes onto the stage and sings. The camera captures various reactions by means of close-ups: we see the deeply moved Fiona, an insecure Marcus, an exasperated Will and a touched Rachel. As some of the audience begin to titter, Will steps in, takes another pupil's guitar and accompanies Marcus both instrumentally and vocally. The audience is mixed between applause and booing. Will draws the attention of the audience to himself and makes them jeer him.

There is a cut to Fiona and Marcus who are leaving the schoolyard, walking down a street. Fiona is deeply moved because of her son's token of love.

Scene Nineteen (1:30:04–1:33:21)
The final scene is set in Will's flat. It begins with a close-up of Will. He is musing: 'Every man is an island. I stand by that. But, clearly, some men are part of island chains. Below the surface of the ocean they're actually connected.' These lines express Will's development from an egotistical, essentially lonely man to a caring and committed person.

It is Christmas. Will, Marcus, Ali, Rachel, Fiona, Ellie and a man who Will met at Amnesty International and who is obviously a kind of blind date for Fiona are all together. The film ends on a notion of togetherness with everyone taking their Christmas dinner plates: there is a close-up of a happy-looking Marcus who says in the form of voice-over narration: 'I don't think couples are the future. You need more than that. You need back-up. The way I see it both Will and I got back-up now.'

Pre-viewing Activities

The following activities may be done after the novel has been read, but before the film has been shown and discussed.

1. Casting

Devise individual profiles for the major characters: Will, Marcus, Fiona, Rachel. These profiles should include:

- what the actors should look like (photos of actors or models in magazines might be brought to class);
- how they should be dressed or made up;
- how else their characters should be depicted (e.g. their manner of speaking, their flats, their cars).

[The students will have formed images of the characters and the location in their heads. Through this activity these images can be transformed into specific shapes. Deciding on, for example, what type of clothes and haircut Will should wear and what his flat should look like will force the students to verbalize their images, thus making them aware of how they have perceived the character. Furthermore, they should decide whether they want to further characterize a given character by 'objective correlatives' that surround the characters, e.g. things they possess.

2. Transforming narrative elements into film language

Re-read Ch. 3 of the novel. As a scriptwriter your task is to 'translate' the reported thought of Marcus into an appropriate form that can be used in the film.

[This task aims to sensitize the students to the difficulties of transforming literary elements into film language. The teacher may have had the students while reading the novel work on the storyboard (cf. p. 32). One problem of adapting the novel is the role of the narration. This could help students consider the possibility of using voice-over for the adaptation of a novel which relies very heavily on the narrative voice for its effect. This activity should not be done in great detail but lead to a classroom discussion about how best to adapt such a chapter, or indeed how to avoid the problems involved.]

While-viewing Activities

It is suggested that prior to watching the film teams are organized that are responsible for one of the following topics:

1. The function and effect of voice-over narration.

[From the guided analysis of the first four chapters the students will have realized that reported thought is a major narrative strategy; they will also know that the narrator sometimes treats Will ironically, sometimes criticizes him and that we as readers soon realize that there are two sides to Will. There is Will, the pretender, and there is Will, the shallow and selfish character. The use of voice-over narration makes it clear to us that Will, the pretender, is supplemented by Will, the cynical observer of himself, and later by Will, the discoverer of his true emotions.

Suitable scenes for voice-over examination are:

- Scene 1: Here Will describes his philosophy of life; he also makes comments on his friends' lifestyle when he visits them, but Will the Non-committer is unified at the end of the episode with his friends when he has to admit he has no interest in children and that he is shallow. Marcus reveals his problems at school and home.
- Scene 2: When Will discovers that Angie has a child, the viewer is confronted with what Will says and what he thinks.
- Scene 7: Marcus talks about the new part of his life starting when Fiona attempts suicide, so the importance of this incident is reinforced for the viewer. It also reveals the two faces of Marcus: there is Marcus, the twelve-year-old boy, and there is Marcus, the precocious child who voices thoughts untypical of someone of his age. Will during the drama of Fiona being taken to the hospital supplements his comment that it was 'horrible' with the comment that 'driving fast behind the ambulance was fantastic'
- Scene 8: Here again Will gives an overview of how he lives. At the restaurant, Will's and Marcus's voice-overs reveal their different views of Fiona's dress style, so the viewer becomes aware of their quite different attitudes and personalities.
- Scene 9: After talking about Fiona and realizing that Marcus is worried by his home life, Will says that he won't make the mistake of asking Marcus about his mother.
- Scene 19: Both Will and Marcus talk about their views of life. The changes from the beginning can be analysed. Will is more connected, while Marcus feels that groups are the future not couples.

So basically the voice-overs illustrate Will's lifestyle, the contrast between his real and projected self, Marcus's problems and the contrast between Will's and Marcus's views on the same issue or incident.]

2. *Striking film elements.*
   Pick five scenes of your choosing and analyse how camera techniques and a given character's state of mind correspond.

[Recommended scenes are:
- Scene 14: Close-ups of Will's face to reveal his embarassment at having to plead with Marcus to pretend he is Will's son. Close-ups of Will and Rachel and then a medium shot of them both to emphasize the feelings between them.
- Scene 15: Over-the-shoulder shots of Will, revealing Rachel's point of view as she tries to inquire about Will's and Marcus's relationship; close-ups of Rachel's face to show her annoyance.
- Scene 16: Twisting bird's-eye view of Marcus to reveal his confusion about his mum; a series of different types of shots and angles at the school reveal Marcus's isolation and the realization that he is committing social suicide. When Will refuses to help Marcus, the camera zooms out away from him, showing him alone in his flat.
- Scene 19: The close-up of Will is then changed as the camera zooms out and others are in Will's flat, revealing how he is no longer isolated or self-sufficient.

3. *Differences between the movie and the book.*
   Concentrate on two or three scenes or chapters that have been left out; compare the endings of the novel and film, and evaluate the changes made in the film. Which do you prefer?

[The following might be mentioned:
- The voice-over narration has replaced reported thought;
- Marcus's seeing his mother in the park is made more credible in the film;
- Fiona's farewell letter plays virtually no role;
- Fiona's educational principles are less important;
- the imagery has been changed: the metaphors of the pyramid (Marcus) and of Will's cracked egg have been replaced by the island metaphor which runs through the whole film;
- the endings are quite different: whereas the film stresses the notion of togetherness, of a joyful Marcus, the novel is more ambiguous, where the focus is more on Marcus's maturity, his growing up and slow distancing from his mother: 'Will knew, then, beyond any shadow of a doubt, that Marcus would be OK.' (p. 254).
- Numerous scenes from the novel have been left out: Marcus's and Ellie's attending a New Year's Eve party, Marcus and Ellie going to Cambridge, Ellie's smashing a shop window, to name but a few.
- The scene with the school concert has been added.
- The fact that Ellie plays an unimportant role in the film.]

Post-viewing Activities

1. *Assessing the film.*
   Write a well-reasoned, critical review. Consider the differences between the film and the book. Evaluate the transformation of the novel into the film and assess the performances of Hugh Grant and of Nicholas Hoult (Marcus).

2. *A talk show about the film.*
   Your teacher will hand you out role cards for a talk show. Imagine you are appearing in a talk show about the film.

[Worksheet 4 (cf. p. 48): To enable the whole course to take part both in the preparation as well as in the realization of the talk show, the following might be considered:
- The class is divided into groups. Individual groups should prepare a role and elect one of their members to play the role. Each participant should decide (with their group) what to say and how to behave.
- Some students could act as phone-in viewers; after a few rounds of views have been exchanged, the moderator allows two or three people to phone in and briefly state their views on matters that have just been spoken about by the members of the panel.
- Some students take notes and do a critical evaluation of the talk show. In this way peer assessment is made possible. Students should evaluate how well the students have performed their roles as well as their linguistic performance. Criticism must be constructive, i.e. specific suggestions for improvement must be made.]

Classroom Tests

Here we present four tests:
a) A review ('Boy Toy', p. 49). The teacher may, instead of the review published here, use one of the reviews to be found at www.cornelsen-teachweb.de/co/bookshelf and www.learnetix.de/bookshelf • Lektüren • About a Boy.
b) An excerpt from the novel ('Excerpt from Chapter Thirty-Six', p. 51).
c) A text about teenage consumerism ('Oh, Da-ad, I Gotta Have One', p. 53)
d) A text about single parents ('Unmarried, with Children', p. 55).
The last two may also be used as additional texts for class disussion rather than as tests.

Boy Toy (p. 49): Suggested Answers

1. The reviewer mentions several aspects of the novel. He writes about the different characters and the content and deals with Will, one of the main characters, in detail. He describes him as a bachelor who doesn't work, who lives a carefree life without any obligations and who only does what he wants. He also speaks about Will's preference for sex with single mothers who, as he puts it, are 'easier to bed'. He briefly deals with the role women play in the novel, but he does not go into detail here.
   Other aspects he mentions are Marcus (the other main character), his mother Fiona and the relationship between Will and Marcus, which is the central relationship in the novel. Marcus is the exact opposite of a normal twelve-year-old, he is very mature and reasonable, knows nothing about the trends his peers indulge in and is an outsider at his school. Initially he very much conforms to the norms his hippie mother encourages: he is a vegetarian, knows nothing about current music and only listens to the music his mother enjoys.
   Woodruff also deals with Marcus's development, which he links to Will's influence and he briefly talks about Marcus's friendship with the rebellious Ellie, who is the exact opposite of Marcus.
2. The writer is right when he says that 'the title may actually be about Will, the child-man, not Marcus, the too-mature kid'. When you hear and read the title of the novel you think of a young boy, a normal teenager. But Marcus is very different from a normal twelve-year-old, he is mature and even precocious and deeply cares about his mother. Often he speaks to her like an adult and they seem to be on equal terms. Indeed, when Fiona is depressed, Marcus talks to her as if he is the parent and she the child.
   Will, on the other hand, is 36 years old but behaves like a teenager. He does not take life seriously, is very self-centred and is only interested in pop culture and women. He is immature and idle, and in this respect he is the opposite of Marcus. Hence the writer seems to be right with his statement. On the other hand, it must be pointed out that the two characters complement each other. Just as Will has taught Marcus how to find his way around in the world and how to find friends, Marcus has taught Will to grow up. Both undergo changes: Marcus becomes the boy and Will the adult. Thus the novel's title might well have been *About Two Boys*.
3. The following should be touched upon or included:
   – Reference to the article you are writing about;
   – Features you agree with;
   – Features you feel should have been dealt with in more detail;
   – Features you felt were ignored (e.g. Marcus's views on the future of the family, the narrative structure).

Excerpt from Chapter 36 (p. 51): Suggested Answers

1. The scene reflects both the allocation of roles typical of their relationship as well as some of the changes that their relationship has undergone.
   Marcus appears to be the more experienced and wiser of the two. Will himself seems to realize this when 'he found himself wanting to talk to Marcus about what it was like to wander about with nothing on', and he is aware of the fact that he is being 'patronized' by Marcus. In this respect, the dialogue reflects the nature of their relationship. On the other hand, the scene shows that both have grown up mentally and emotionally. Will has learned that he does need other people and their love and affection, and Marcus has emotionally adjusted himself to his patchwork family.
2. The changes in question are clearly expressed by the images of the cracked egg and the human pyramid. As Will has opened up to the world, has started to relate to people emotionally and to commit himself, he has begun to leave behind his desire to remain immature and to face responsibilities for himself and others. Likewise, Marcus has learned to relate to people; he no longer withdraws and is no longer an outsider. He has adjusted to his new surroundings and, as the metaphor of the pyramid suggests, wishes to experience mutual dependability and trust. Furthermore, the metaphor suggests that he has become emotionally stable and is no longer afraid of losing his mother.
3. [Students should observe the rules of diary writing. Their entries should reflect their analysis of the scene, i.e. they could reveal a Marcus who is still patronizing, and who is becoming more self-con-

fident. They might use the metaphor of the pyramid and place Will and Marcus in that pyramid. The task is linguistically demanding and presupposes that the students are familiar with creative writing assignments.]

Oh Da-ad, I Gotta Have One (p. 53):
Suggested Answers

1. Formerly, children were happy with a lot less. They wore the clothes their parents bought them. They would play games at birthday parties, accept presents that were neither exciting nor thrilling and eat very straightforward food.
   Nowadays, children demand to be given designer clothes, replicas of their favourite football team outfits. They expect more treats at birthday parties. They are generally viewed by commerce as being consumers.
2. The writer is critical of the new trends in youth consumerism. He contrasts how children would expect less 30 years ago and explains the rise in demand to parental guilt, as parents have less time; this indicates that youth consumerism is linked to a breakdown in family values and ties. He uses the word 'epidemic' to describe parental guilt, and refers to parents as 'indulgent' and to their 'indulgence'. The children themselves are simply referred to as 'spoilt bastards'. He describes the need to keep up with other children's possessions as 'excruciating moral pressure', which is meant ironically. The makers of football kits 'seek to make as much profit as they can'. Adjectives like 'eye-watering', 'extravagant' and 'snazziest' all underline the negative attitude of the writer to his topic.
3. Much will depend on when Fiona writes the letter. If it is towards the beginning of the novel, Fiona will obviously take the same view as the writer and deplore the idea that children behave like sheep, each following the other. She might also question whether parents are being responsible by encouraging their children to behave in such a way. Finally, she might refer to her educational principles, which she believes have contributed to Marcus's well-being.
   If Fiona writes the letter after the events in the novel, she might want to compromise a little, and say how she discovered that, however deplorable the situation is, nevertheless teenagers do need to feel part of a group. She could add that her son, Marcus, now feels much happier following some of the trends that his peers follow, but that he is aware that due to her low income she cannot indulge his every whim.

Unmarried, with Children (p. 55).
Suggested Answers

1. They deal with the following aspects: the demographic changes concerning single parenthood; the role of the single mother in society; and the effect of single parenthood on children.
2. The writers try to adopt a neutral position. They introduce the topic by referring to a well-known soap from the 1950s, and say how the soap would look today.
   They then give the figures that show why they feel the soap would look different today.
   They try to shed light on the way single parents live and show that it is not just poor people who are single parents, as used to be largely the case.
   They offer a variety of viewpoints: Some of those questioned, e.g. Stephanie Coontz, say society just has to accept the new family model; others, e.g. Susan Brown and Robert Rector, say that children brought up in single-parent households will suffer more than those brought up in married households; while Larry Bumpass says that there is little difference between the different types of families.
   So, the writers try and present a balanced view.
3. Marcus, Ellie and Ali are being raised by their mothers. Marcus is a weird child, and at the beginning blames his mother for his being weird. But when his father is introduced, it is far from clear that Marcus would have been any different if he had been brought up by both his parents. However, it is Marcus's view that two is not enough; but rather than believing that couples are the future, he believes in people helping each other. Ellie is a strong-minded person with a lack of self-esteem. Ali seems to hate the idea of anyone taking his mother away from him. So by and large, none of the children are emotionally very stable, but there are no children living with both parents to compare them with. One must also consider the fact that *About a Boy* is not really a sociological study, but an entertaining novel in which the author makes use of caricature to amuse the reader.

How to Give a Presentation

Presentation skills are not just important for the classroom but for your future career. Being able to put across information effectively in a way that interests your listeners is a vital part of communication. Here are a few tips on how to give an effective presentation.

Organizing your team work

- Allocate areas of responsibility: who does what, when and how. Decide if you want to rotate the responsibilities or if they should stay with one person. Find out who is best suited to deal with a given task.
- Keep minutes of each meeting. Jot down your progress and specify tasks yet to be done.
- Develop a strategy how to deal with your topic. Naturally, all of you must read the entire novel. However, your focus of attention while reading it may be different, as each of you may pay attention to different aspects.
- Collect paragraphs from the novel that refer to your topic. Do a collage of these quotations. In this way you have all the key passages in front of you and it will be easier for you to analyse them.
- Evaluate these passages. If you have difficulty expressing what you want to say, jot down ideas, words and phrases on your protocol paper. Your teacher will help you.
- Prepare an outline for your oral presentation. Discuss this outline with your teacher.
- Think of ways to make your presentation more interesting, e.g. by using visuals, sound, jokes, etc. Can you add creativity to your presentation, e.g. would reading out a letter or a diary entry written by a character, or a role play throw light on your topic?
- Write your analysis and hand it in to your teacher in a folder.

Presenting Your Findings

- Start by explaining your topic and how your talk is structured.
- Pay attention to your body language: stand straight and face the audience, keeping eye contact with them. Speak clearly and slowly; use simple vocabulary.
- Use visuals or handouts to hold your audience's attention.
- Do not read your presentation. Make it seem natural.
- Summarize the important points at the end of your talk.
- Thank your audience for their attention and ask whether they have any questions.

How to Write a Book Review

Writing a book review about the novel you have read in class is a rewarding way of reacting to the novel. Too often, students, however, write a book review without planning it carefully beforehand. Here are a few guidelines for you.

Introduction

Start off with information about the writer and his earlier work or, if this is not possible, begin with a quote that will catch the reader's attention. It is also important to mention the novel you are writing about.

Step 1:

Write a brief summary of the book in about 100 words. Be sure that your summary makes sense to a reader who may not know the book.

Step 2:

Present the main characters. Say something about their personality traits. State your reasons if and why you identify with a given character. Mention whether the writer makes you believe in them as real people.

Step 3:

Note down what in your opinion is the 'message' of the novel. It is not always easy to describe the message. Therefore consider the following:

How is the end different from the beginning?

Is there a quote or paragraph which you think contains the essence of the novel?

Step 4 (optional):

Relate the book to other novels of a similar theme that you know. What is unique about this novel?

Step 5:

Place the book in its cultural context.

Step 6:

Assess the book. What are its strengths and weaknesses? Consider the plot, the structure, the characters, the ending, the language. Support your views with references to the novel.

Step 7:

Either recommend the book or advise against reading it. Make sure that your final judgement is logically developed and well-reasoned.

Introduction

Read the following extract from *About a Boy*.

I'm a single father. I have a two-year-old boy. I'm a single father. I have a two-year-old boy. I'm a single father. I have a two-year-old boy. However many times Will told himself this, he could always find some reason that prevented him from believing it; in his own head – not the place that counted the most, but important nevertheless – he didn't feel like a parent. He was too young, too old, too stupid, too smart, too groovy, too impatient, too selfish, too careless, too careful (whatever the contraceptive circumstances of the woman he was seeing, he always, always used a Durex, even in the days before you had to), he didn't know enough about kids, he went out too often, he drank too much, he took too many drugs. When he looked in the mirror, he didn't, couldn't, see a dad, especially a single dad.

He was trying to see a single dad in the mirror because he had run out of single mums to sleep with; in fact, Angie had so far proved to be both the beginning and the end of his supply. It was all very well deciding that single mums were the future, that there were millions of sad, Julie Christie-like waifs just dying for his call, but the frustrating truth was that he didn't have any of their phone numbers. Where did they hang out?

It took him longer than it should have done to realize that, by definition, single mothers had children, and children, famously, prevented one from hanging out anywhere. He had made a few gentle, half-hearted enquiries of friends and acquaintances, but had so far failed to make any real headway; the people he knew either didn't know any single mothers, or were unwilling to effect the necessary introductions due to Will's legendarily poor romantic track record. But now he had found the ideal solution to this unexpected dearth of prey. He had invented a two-year-old son called Ned and had joined a single parents' group.

Most people would not have bothered to go to these lengths to indulge a whim, but Will quite often bothered to do things that most people wouldn't bother to do, simply because he had the time to bother. Doing nothing all day gave him endless opportunities to dream and scheme and pretend to be something he wasn't. He had, after a fit of remorse following a weekend of extreme self-indulgence, volunteered to work in a soup kitchen, and even though he never actually reported for duty, the phone call had allowed him to pretend, for a couple of days, that he was the kind of guy who might. And he had thought about VSO and filled in the forms, and he had cut out an advert in the local paper about teaching slow learners to read, and he had contacted estate agents about opening a restaurant and then a bookshop …

The point was that if you had a history of pretending, then joining a single parent group when you were not a single parent was neither problematic nor particularly scary. If it didn't work out, then he'd just have to try something else. It was no big deal.

Marcus: A Character Profile

Fill in the following worksheet with information about Marcus that you have obtained in the first four chapters.

Facts about his life

Relationships with others

Characteristics

Marcus

Problems

Examples of his use of language

How I view Marcus

Will: A Character Profile

Fill in the following worksheet with information about Will that you have obtained in the first four chapters.

Facts about his life

Relationships with others

Characteristics

Will

Problems

Examples of his use of language

How I view Marcus

A Talk Show about the Film

Role card: The host of the talk show

You moderate the talkshow and are responsible for the procedure, i.e. you say whose turn it is to speak, you decide how to organize the discussion (for example, you choose the first things that will be discussed) and you make sure that all participants have an equal share in the discussion.
As the host, you must be polite, friendly and neutral, i.e. you shouldn't take sides.

Role card: Paul Weitz, the director

You are proud of the film and are convinced that it is a great film. You are sure that you did justice to the novel, i.e. that you kept its central ideas and transformed them into the medium film. You should be able to illustrate this with examples from the film.
You are self-confident and even, perhaps, a bit arrogant.

Role card: Hugh Grant, actor

You are the star of the film and radiate that fact. You should stress the excellent cooperation with the director and the other members of the crew. So think of one or two examples to underline your point. It is up to you to decide if you want to be critical of one or two aspects ('I might have done this or that better') of your performance and if you want to express a bit of irony. You should also say something about the role of Will, the extent to which you identified with the figure.

Role card: Toni Collette, actress

You played the difficult role of Fiona. You should say something about Fiona as a character, how you saw her and why it was difficult for you to play that role. However, you should be very content with your performance and be able to underline that with examples from your acting.

Role card: Film critic of the *Guardian*

You wrote a very critical review of the film. You think that Hugh Grant was a wrong choice, because he was too likeable as Will. Also Grant is too good-looking to play the character convincingly. Furthermore, you find fault with the use of voice-over narration. To your mind it was used excessively. You would have wished the director had translated some of the central images ('all men are an island') into images in the film. Ultimately you believe the voice-over narration shows a lack of creativity on the director's part. Be prepared to back up your criticism with one or two examples from the film. Remember that a critic that wants to be convincing speaks in a friendly tone and does not use any harsh language.

A Review of the Novel

Text

Boy Toy

This Week's Winner for the most obvious fictional character name goes to Will Freeman, the protagonist of Nick Hornby's *About A Boy*. A superficial, jobless, early-30s fellow who lives from half-hour to half-hour with no emotional ties to restrict him, Will values his ability to make decisions based solely on his immediate impulses. It's Will's will, dammit, and nobody had better tell Freeman he can't be free, man.

Thankfully, the rest of Hornby's book isn't nearly as obnoxiously clever. Oh, it has its moments, like when Will starts attending SPAT groups (that's Single Parents-Alone Together) so that he can pick up on single mothers, whom he discovers are even easier to bed and dump than swinging bachelorettes. Or when the son of one of those women catches on to Will's scheme, and uses this knowledge to blackmail Will into becoming his father figure (thus forming the basis for the book's story). But mostly, *About A Boy* is a pleasant, satisfying read, the kind that touches sentimental nerves even as it struggles to be cool.

With *About A Boy*, it's as if Hornby had acquired a girlfriend and some Prozac since his last outing. Hornby's prose is much happier than before (even while it keeps hitting the hip, cynical notes); and the fixation on girlfriends past and present is gone, gone, gone – women play prominent roles in the novel, but aren't a major concern for the main character. Instead, the story centers on the relationship between Will and Marcus, the previously mentioned son of one of the SPAT mothers.

Basically, Marcus adopts Will. Marcus's mother, Fiona, is an uptight hippie vegetarian who won't let Marcus indulge in any of society's frivolities because she believes in total non-conformity. As a result, Marcus is an extremely awkward twelve-year-old. He dresses like hell or as Hornby, a Brit, would say, he wears 'really crap' clothes. He doesn't understand sarcasm. And the kids at his new London school harass him on a daily basis. What's worse, Fiona is on the verge of suicide, constantly breaking into bouts of sobbing for no apparent reason. Between school and home, Marcus is miserable.

So even though Will couldn't be farther from an ideal father-figure, Marcus decides to turn him into one. Actually, it's precisely because Will is such a childish man that he's the ideal friend for Marcus, who is growing up too fast and needs to learn how to be a twelve-year-old. And Will is the perfect teacher: He shows Marcus how to dress like everybody else, how to let out a sardonic 'ha ha' to prime I-couldn't-care-less-effect, and even how to listen to Nirvana (a stark contrast from the Joni Mitchell albums Marcus's mother force-feeds him). Here we have another instance of Hornby's cleverness: The title, *About A Boy*, may actually be about Will the child-man, not Marcus the too-mature kid.

One of the best aspects of *About A Boy* is its continuous refusal to head off in sappy directions. There are plenty of opportunities for Hornby to hook Will up with Marcus's mother, or to involve Marcus in teenage romance (with a rebellious, butt-kicking Gothy chick), or kill off characters to get melodramatic. Hornby resists all those temptations, opting for the dry ins-and-outs of day-to-day existence, where things are rarely tied up neatly. He never tries for profound meanings – like Will, he seems embarrassed by the whole enterprise – but he really nails the smaller observations. *About A Boy* is more self-consciously smart than it is brilliant, but that's all it needs in order to be entertaining and wryly sweet.

(By Zachary Woodruff, *Tucson Weekly*, 8 September, 1998; 597 words)

9 *bachelorette:* an unmarried woman who lives alone **13** *Prozac:* brand name of antidepressant medication

Tasks

1. Point out which aspects of the novel are emphasized by the reviewer.
2. 'The title may actually be about Will, the child-man, not Marcus, the too-mature kid.' Do you agree with this statement. Use information from the review and the novel to support your view.
3. Write a letter to the editor of the newspaper, in which you critically discuss this review.

Excerpt from Chapter Thirty-Six

It was strange; Will missed him. Since the egg had cracked Will had found himself wanting to talk to Marcus about what it was like to wander about with nothing on, feeling scared of everything and everybody, because Marcus was the only person in the world who might be able to offer him advice; but Marcus – the old Marcus, anyway – was disappearing.

'Are you going to marry my mum?' Ali asked out of the blue, during one of their pre-cinema fast-food meals. Marcus looked up from his chips with interest.

'I dunno,' Will mumbled. He had thought about it a lot, but could never quite make himself believe that he was entitled to ask her; every time he stayed over at her house he felt impossibly blessed, and he didn't want to do anything that would endanger his sense of privilege. Sometimes he hardly even dared ask her when he could see her again; asking her whether she was willing to spend the rest of her life with him seemed to be pushing it.

'I used to want him to marry my mum,' Marcus said cheerfully. Will was suddenly seized with the desire to pour his boiling-point fast-food coffee down the front of Marcus's shirt.

'Did you?' said Ali.

'Yeah. For some reason I thought it would sort everything out. Your mum's different, though. She's more together than mine.'

'Do you still want him to marry your mum?'

'Don't I get a say in this?' Will asked.

'Naah,' said Marcus, ignoring Will's interruption. 'See, I don't think that's the right way.'

'Why not?'

'Because … You know when they do those human pyramids? That's the sort of model for living I'm looking at now.'

'What are you talking about, Marcus?' Will asked him. It wasn't a rhetorical question.

'You're safer as a kid if everyone's friends. When people pair off … I don't know. It's more insecure. Look at it now. Your mum and my mum get on OK.' It was true. Fiona and Rachel saw each other regularly now, to Will's agonizing discomfort. 'And Will sees her, and I see you, and Ellie and Zoe, and Lindsey and my dad. I've got it sorted now. If your mum and Will get together, you think you're safe, but you're not, because they'll split up, or Will will go mad or something.'

Ali nodded sagely. Will's urge to scald had been replaced by an urge to shoot Marcus and then turn the gun on himself.

'What if Rachel and I don't split up? What if we stay together forever?'

'Fine. Great. Prove it. I just don't think couples are the future.'

'Oh, well thank you ... Einstein.' Will had wanted his comeback to be sharper than that. He wanted to think of some sort of socio-cultural marriage expert whose name two twelve-year-olds would instantly recognize, but Einstein was all he could come up with. He knew it wasn't right.

'What's he got to do with it?'

'Nothing,' Will mumbled. Marcus looked at him pityingly. 'And don't patronize me.'

'What does patronize mean?' Marcus asked, in all seriousness. So there it was. Will was being patronized by someone who wasn't even old enough to understand what the word meant.

'It means, don't treat me like an idiot.'

Marcus looked at him as if to say, well, how else can I treat you? And Will had every sympathy. He was really struggling to maintain the age gap now: Marcus's air of authority, the been-there-done-that tone in his voice, was so convincing that Will didn't know how to argue with him. He didn't want to either. He hadn't lost all face yet; there was still a tiny patch left, about the size of a small scab, and he wanted to keep it.

(From: Nick Hornby, *About a Boy*, 703 words)

Tasks

1. Briefly describe the relationship between Will and Marcus as depicted in this excerpt.
2. Analyse how Will's and Marcus's attitudes towards people have changed.
   Pay special attention to the imagery associated with each.
3. Imagine you are Marcus. Write a diary entry in which you comment on the changes in Will.

Oh, Da-ad, I Gotta Have One

After the match against Manchester United on Saturday, young boys queued with their fathers on the first floor of the Chelsea Megastore at Stamford Bridge, waiting for their last chance to be photographed with the FA Cup at £15 a time.

Most of them were wearing the full replica Chelsea strip, which had set their parents back £29.99 for the shirt, £16.99 for the shorts and £7.99 for the socks (all prices are for children's sizes). Some of the boys wore Nike trainers – not much change there from £50. The average cost of each boy's outfit, including anoraks and underwear, was probably about £100. The most expensively dressed wore clothes that cost £200. There was an awful lot of money and parental indulgence in that queue. There in the crush was a boy of about nine, gazing adoringly at a Chelsea FC bicycle, painted in the club's colours and priced at £199.99. 'Oh dad. Da-ad, I gotta have one. But da-ad, Matthew's got one.'

Chelsea and all the other Premier League football clubs are now under investigation by the Office of Fair Trading, which suspects them of keeping prices of their official merchandise artificially high by cutting off supplies to retailers who sell at a discount.

The wonder is not that the clubs seek to make as much profit as they can from their replica kits but that so many parents are prepared to spend these eyewatering sums on their young, faithfully coming back for the latest version every time the teams change their strip. [...] But it is not only at the Chelsea Megastore that parents are lavishing expensive presents on their young. All over the country, an entire generation of 'spoilt bastards' is being reared, demanding and receiving ever more extravagant treats from their increasingly indulgent parents. Much of the explanation for this new generosity is the dramatic rise in incomes over the lifetimes of the current generation of schoolchildren's parents. But a big part of it, too, is an epidemic of parental guilt. With more and more mothers at work, and fathers working longer hours, parents are seeing less of their children – and many choose to compensate with their wallets at the weekend for their absence during the week. The trend towards spending ever greater sums on the young is driven by relentless peer-pressure at school, ruthlessly exploited by the manufacturers of clothes, computers, sporting goods and games.

In the Fifties and Sixties, even the children of quite rich parents were content to wear whatever clothes their parents chose to put them in. It would not have occurred to them to look at labels, still less to insist on clothes by a particular designer.

Today's generation, particularly in towns, is acutely fashion-conscious, and the child in the T-shirt and gym-shoes from Woolies is made to feel deeply inferior to his schoolmate in the latest Umbro football-strip, the Nike trainers or the Dr Martens.

Birthday presents were always status-symbols to children. But whereas 30 years ago, the highest status might have been conferred by a top-of-the-range Airfix model, a pair of roller-skates or a Corgi Cadillac, with wheels that actually turned, today nothing less will do than the latest and best computer-games system or the snazziest in-line skates on the market, with all the trimming.

Over the past 10 years or so, parents have found that it is not enough to splash out on a one-off purchase of a computer-system. No sooner have they plugged it in than a new one, infinitely more sophisticated, comes on the market and they are immediately under excruciating moral pressure to upgrade.

In the old days, a birthday party for a 10-year-old would involve a few games of pass-the-parcel and musical bumps, a plate of jelly, a slice of cake – and a magician if the child was jolly lucky. Today, increasing numbers of children expect to take a party of friends to a theme park (call that £200). Others may settle for the go-kart-track, at £150-an-hour for a party of ten, with a meal at McDonald's or Pizzaland afterwards.

(From: *The Daily Telegraph,* 6 March, 1998; 680 words)

3 *FA:* Football Association **4/16** *replica strip/kit:* copy of the clothes footballers wear during a match **10** *Chelsea FC:* Chelsea Football Club **12** *Premier League:* England's first division professional football league **33** *Woolies:* the department store Woolworths **34** *Umbro:* (brandname) sportswear **34** *Dr. Martens:* (brandname) shoes

Tasks

1. Describe children's attitude towards consumer goods then and now.
2. Analyse the writer's attitude towards the present generation of young consumers and show how this attitude is reflected in his language.
3. This article was published in the same year as the novel *About a Boy*. Write a letter to the editor from Fiona's point of view in which you comment on the article.

Unmarried, with Children

Just imagine what would happen if June and Ward Cleaver were negotiating family life these days. The scenario might go something like this: they meet at the office (she's in marketing; he's in sales) and move in together after dating for a couple of months. A year later June gets pregnant. What to do? Neither feels quite ready to make it legal and there's no pressure from their parents, all of whom are divorced and remarried themselves. So little Wally is welcomed into the world with June's last name on the birth certificate. A few years later June gets pregnant again with the Beav. Ward's ambivalent about secondtime fatherhood and moves out, but June decides to go ahead on her own. In her neighborhood, after all, single motherhood is no big deal; the lesbians down the street adopted kids from South America and the soccer mom next door is divorced with a live-in boyfriend.

Figures released last week from the 2000 Census show that this postmodern June would be almost as mainstream as the 1950s version. The number of families headed by single mothers has increased 25 percent since 1990, to more than 7.5 million households. Contributing to the numbers are a high rate of divorce and out-of-wedlock births. For most of the past decade, about a third of all babies were born to unmarried women, compared with 3.8 percent in 1940. Demographers now predict that more than half of the youngsters born in the 1990s will spend at least part of their childhood in a single-parent home. [...] In contrast, married couples raising children – the 'Leave It to Beaver' model – account for less than a quarter of all households.

Demographers and politicians will likely spend years arguing about what this all means and whether the shifts are real or just numerical flukes. But one thing everyone does agree on is that single mothers are now a permanent and significant page in America's diverse family album. 'We can encourage, pressure, preach and give incentives to get people to marry,' says Stephanie Coontz, author of *The Way We Never Were* and a family historian at the Evergreen State College in Olympia, Wash. 'But we still have to deal with the reality that kids are going to be raised in a variety of ways, and we have to support all kinds of families with kids.'

This new breed of single mothers doesn't fit the old stereotype of an unwed teen on welfare. She's still likely to be financially insecure, but she could be any age and any race. The median age for unmarried mothers is the late 20s, and the fastest-growing category is white women. She may be divorced or never-married. Forty percent are living with men who may be the fathers of one or more of their children; as the Census numbers also showed, there's been nearly a 72-percent increase in the number of cohabiting couples, many of whom bring along children from previous relationships. She may also be a single mother by choice. Unwed motherhood has lost much of its stigma [...]. 'Twenty years ago middle-class women believed it took a man to have a child, but that's no longer true,' says Rosanna Hertz, chair of the women's studies department at Wellesley College. 'We've reached a watershed moment.' [...]

Even under the very best of conditions, single motherhood is a long, hard journey for both mother and children. No one really knows the long-term consequences for youngsters who grow up in these new varieties of single-parent and cohabiting homes. Much of the research in the past on alternative living arrangements has concentrated on children of divorce, who face very different issues than youngsters whose parents have chosen to be single from the start or are cohabiting with their children's fathers or other partners. 'We need to start paying attention to how these kids living in cohabiting homes are doing, says Susan Brown, a sociologist at Bowling Green State University in Ohio. 'All the evidence we have suggests that they are not doing too well.'

Single mothers in general have less time for each individual child than two parents and cohabiting relationships are less stable than marriages. That means that children living in these families are more likely to grow up with a revolving set of adults in their lives. And the offspring of single parents are more likely to skip the altar themselves, thus perpetuating the pattern of their childhood. 'Children living outside marriage are seven times more likely to experience poverty and are 17 times more likely to end up on welfare and to have a propensity for emotional problems, discipline problems, early pregnancy and abuse,' says Robert Rector, a senior research fellow at the Heritage Foundation, a conservative think tank. 'It can be a recipe for disaster.'

'The average kid in a single-parent family looks much the same emotionally as children who grow up in the most-conflicted two-parent homes,' says Larry Bumpass, a sociologist at the University of Wisconsin. But, he adds, 'the average is not the script written for every child. The outcomes are not all negative; it's just a matter of relative probability … the majority will do just fine.'

(From: Barbara Kantrowitz, Pat Wingert, *Newsweek*, 28 May, 2001; 865 words)

1 *June and Ward Cleaver:* characters in the 1950s US family soap *Leave It to Beaver* **1** *negotiate sth.:* deal with sth. **12** *mainstream:* normal **14** *out-of-wedlock:* to parents who are not married **16** *demographer:* person who studies changes in the population **20** *fluke:* unlikely happening which is due to chance **22** *incentive:* (often financial) form of encouragement **26** *breed:* type **26** *unwed:* unmarried **31** *cohabit:* live together **35** *watershed:* period of important change **48** *skip sth.:* leave sth. out **48** *perpetuate sth.:* make sth. continue to exist **50** *propensity:* natural tendency

Tasks

1. Point out which aspects of single parenthood are dealt with by the writers of this article.
2. What view do the writers take of single parenthood?
3. Relate the findings in this article to *About a Boy*. To what extent are they reflected in the novel?